D0782782

PLAINS & PEAKS

PLAINS & PEAKS

A WILDERNESS OUTFITTER'S STORY

by
Tory Taylor

HOMESTEAD PUBLISHING
Moose, Wyoming

Copyright © 1994 by Tory Taylor
All rights reserved. No portion of this book can be
copied, electronically or by other means without
permission.

Library of Congress Catalog Card Number 93-81204
ISBN 0-943972-30-2

Printed in the United States of America.
The text of this book is composed in Granjon. This type font
was produced in 1931 by George Jones and was named for the
16th century printer Robert Granjon. The letterforms are based
on the 1592 Egenolff-Berner specimen sheet printed with the
type of Claude Garamond.
Composition and production by Homestead Publishing.
Book design by Carl Schreier.

Published by
HOMESTEAD PUBLISHING
Box 193, Moose, Wyoming 83012

First Edition

CONTENTS

FOREWORD

This book represents my third attempt at putting my hunting and outdoor adventures on paper, experiences that span over 35 years. The backdrop setting is the spectacular Rocky Mountains, where remnant islands of prime big-game habitat still exist. How long these islands will stand before being further eroded depends upon people who care about wildlife and wildlands. Just as this book is in the interested readers' hands, the future of wildlife and wildlands lies in the hands of concerned, committed individuals like you and me.

A few of these stories are favorites that first appeared in my previous book, "Hunting on Big Game Trails." However, most of the stories in this collection have never before seen the light of day.

I have tried to capture the meaning and satisfaction of hunting. This is something difficult to do because hunting means many things to many people; neither I nor anyone else can speak for every hunter. It is a task similar to one person trying to define a universal religion for all people. If, however, my writing gives someone insight and understanding into hunting, I will consider my work a success. In these days of an increasing anti-hunting movement, hunters, fishermen, and sportsmen need to re-evaluate the portrait they paint to the public. There are a number of good reasons for hunting, but they generally are not stated in a balanced, reasonable forum. I hope these hunting tales set the mood for constructive discussions about the future of wildlife management in our country and around the world.

My best to you during your days in the field, and remember to take a kid along next time you go hunting or fishing.

Tory Taylor
Dubois, Wyoming

Chapter One
Elk Hunting in the High Country

 Another year of chasing dollars had passed and autumn approached. It was time to think about trying to put a freezer around an elk. I contacted my favorite hunting partner; we discussed the details and organized the hunt. It had taken me years of searching to find a good hunting partner because I had demanding standards. I looked for someone who could handle the rough and desolate places I often hunt. My partner had to know horses and be efficient with camp chores. I wanted someone who was a dedicated sportsman and careful with a rifle. Above all, a good hunting partner would share my reverence of wildlife and my love for the mountains.

When I finally met the person who possessed all of these qualifications, I married her. Meredith became my wife, best friend, and favorite hunting partner. Early on, we put every cent we earned into building our new home. I borrowed a packhorse from my brother, as buying and feeding horses was out of the question for us. Meredith and I planned to walk to one of our favorite hunting areas and pack a light camp on the horse. My brother and a friend decided to meet us a few days later and help pack out an elk if we killed one.

Eight inches of crusted snow made walking difficult and slow. We camped early the first day, even though we were only half way to base camp. We laid our bedroll out between canvas covers where we enjoyed looking at the bright stars in the clear, cold sky and listening to the quiet of the mountains.

Sometime in the night, I was awakened by the sound of horses approaching our camp. A group of hunters had seen the coals of our campfire and rode over to find out who we were. I recognized the voice that called out and immediately raised my hackles. The voice belonged to one of the most lawless slob hunters ever to call himself an outfitter. He was glad to hear we were looking for elk since his clients and he were hunting for bighorn sheep.

He told us about the vast herds of elk they had ridden through that evening and was surprised we had not seen them. His report did not interest me because I knew the man would rather lie than tell the truth. I bid them goodnight as they rode away, but I don't think the outfitter heard me say I hoped he would break his leg. I thought it was appropriate for the man to be out at night since skunks are nocturnal varmints.

Around noon of the second day, we waded across a knee-deep stream. Meredith was the first to roll up her pants and sling her boots around her neck. She started wading the slow-moving, icy stream, then let out a painful, "Ouch!" A paper-thin skim of invisible ice was on the surface of the water and made thin cuts in her shins as she waded. It was like wading through razor blades.

"Thanks for breaking the trail for me and the horse, honey," I said cheerfully. In reply, Meredith threw a rock and splashed water on me.

Later that day, we camped in a meadow near elk country. Toward evening, we found a vantage point at timberline and sat shivering in a cold wind, hoping an elk would appear. Fresh tracks were disappointingly sparce and no animal showed itself. We decided to try a different area the next day.

We both had elk licenses and carried rifles but had already decided we would shoot only one elk. In addition to the antelope already in our freezer, one elk would provide enough meat for us for the year. Meredith had never shot an elk, and I hoped she would be the one to fill the freezer.

During the hunt, I tried out my new philosophy about meat and trophy hunting: I vowed never to shoot a bull for its head unless it was bigger than any I had ever shot. If I did not see a larger bull, I would try to shoot a dry cow for meat.

I struck upon this idea after observing antelope hunters. Time after time, I had watched or heard about antelope hunters who passed up bunch after bunch of antelope with plentiful barren does, and then shoot a small buck. These people were not meat hunters: They often passed easy shots at tasty dry does and tried ridiculous running shots at small bucks. Nor were they trophy hunters: Year after year, the heads of the small bucks they shot ended up at the local landfill. I also noticed these hunters often were the same ones who complained there were no trophy bucks left. They never stopped to consider what might happen if they cropped the barren does and left the small bucks to live for a few years. I decided it made sense to shoot an old, dry cow elk if I didn't see a big bull. I would be happy to let the productive cows, calves, and young bulls grow.

On the third day, we walked over a high alpine ridge and moved our camp to another drainage. Sometime around midday, we descended a faint game trail just above timberline. I looked with great interest at the fresh elk tracks and numerous droppings along the trail. We led the packhorse down the game trail and through the timber for nearly a mile before we found what we were looking for. There, a small meadow that once was the bottom of a beaver pond was nestled between two ridges covered with black timber. It now had a clear stream running through it and made an excellent campsite. A stand of trees at the edge of the meadow provided a snug, sheltered spot for our camp.

From the cooking fire, I watched the picketed packhorse graze. A few steps in the opposite direction, I collected ice-cold water from the stream. It wasn't a bad setup.

Late that afternoon, Meredith posted herself in a clump of trees at the edge of a large, grassy park. I walked a quarter of a mile above her and found a promising spot at timberline to look for elk. A cold, cutting wind had begun to blow from the north. I waited patiently for an elk, while slowly freezing to death. I wore all the clothes I had brought, but they were no barrier from the icy wind that chilled me to the bone. Rocking slowly from foot to foot, I tried to keep the blood circulating, but it was useless. How I hoped to hear a report from Meredith's rifle, but no report came. It was nearly dark when I decided to glass a barren ridge nearly a mile away. On the ridge, a long line of elk filed out of the trees and began to graze. Too far away for a late-evening stalk, I remained at my post until dark, hoping for a straggler—which never came.

The next morning, we split at camp. Meredith planned to wait until daylight and hunt the park she had watched the previous evening. I wanted to leave camp just as the eastern sky began to glow and at first light be near the barren ridge where I had seen the elk grazing. It was a beautiful, clear morning when I walked from camp. The wind had stopped and stillness reigned over the dark forest. A cow elk barked across the valley. Then the forest became absolutely silent. No breeze whispered in the pines, no squirrel chattered, no coyote barked, no bird called. If it had not been such a peaceful silence, it would have seemed almost spooky.

Suddenly, I had the eery feeling I was no longer alone, and the hair on my neck crawled. I froze and concentrated on my surroundings but only a sixth sense relayed any message. A huge, house-sized boulder twenty yards to my left seemed to attract my attention. I moved a few steps closer until it was silhouetted against the early-morning sky. The rock resembled a huge buffalo, and I stared at it for some time, trying to figure out what had caught my attention. I was a hunter and believed only what I saw, yet somehow I was compelled to speak, "Grandfather, walk with me."

With those words, the eerie feeling suddenly vanished and common noises again came from the woods. I turned and continued toward the ridge.

As I approached the scattered parks and narrow strips of trees on the ridge, a bull elk bugled a quarter of a mile in front of me. I smiled to myself, knowing the elk were near. I slowly moved toward the bugling bull and looked in all directions after each step. New tracks in the snow, fresh droppings, and the strong scent of elk were everywhere. I eased to the edge of a final strip of wind-stunted trees and carefully peeked through.

Elk were everywhere I looked. The closest were less than a hundred yards away, while some were a thousand yards above on a steep hillside. Two hundred and fifty yards in front of me stood a fair-sized, six-point bull with several cows and calves. I watched as the bull bugled time after time at a smaller bull that cautiously circled the herdmaster. Tree limbs provided a solid rest for my rifle as I held the crosshairs on the the bugling bull's lungs. Knowing that the bull's rack was not as big as the six-point antlers on my wall at home, I never released the safety of my rifle. The bull lived to echo his bugle from the mountain slopes.

Then, from the corner of my eye, I saw movement thirty yards to my left. Slowly I turned my eyes in that direction to see a small bunch of cows and several calves grazing toward me. Easing into shooting position and releasing the safety, I watched several pairs of cows and calves move twenty yards in front of my rifle's muzzle. A calfless, dark-colored cow was the last of the bunch, and I picked a spot just behind her shoulder with the crosshairs. I suddenly thought about the words of an old hunter and friend: "When I was young and able to hunt, I'd always try to shoot an animal just behind the jaw." I had never felt confident enough to try that kind of shot before, but this seemed like a perfect chance. Moving the crosshairs an inch behind the grazing cow's ear, I squeezed the trigger. The cow fell hard and died instantly. The remaining elk trotted into a milling bunch before they moved into protective timber.

Later, on my return to camp for the packhorse, I paused beside the huge rock that earlier had reminded me of a buffalo and pondered the feeling I had experienced there. I could find no explanation. As I turned, I happily called over my shoulder, "Thank you," and continued on to camp.

❦

The following year, Meredith and I camped next to a large willow-covered meadow nearly two miles from where I had ear-shot the cow elk. We had packed in a few days before elk season in order to set up a comfortable camp and relax before we hunted. How wonderful it was to be in the mountains once more!

My yearnings to return to the high country had always been strong, but several times I wondered if the effort of packing in twenty miles for elk was worth the time and trouble. There were elk a lot closer to home. As soon as we set up our camp, however, my doubts and troubles seemed to disappear. I looked at the horses happily grazing, heard Meredith rattling pans on the stove, watched a golden eagle gliding over the towering mountaintops, saw trout darting in the clear stream at my feet, smelled the pine forest as the breeze swayed the treetops, and marveled at a brilliant dragonfly perching on the track of a moose at the edge of a beaver dam.

I let out a little laugh and said to myself, "Yeah, it's worth it."

As long as there is country like that to go to and as long as I have strength enough to get to it, it is no doubt worth it. We had become a little more prosperous during the preceding year and had acquired four horses. One was a gentle old mare who served as the kingpin of our outfit. The other three were rookies with good natures and potential, but definitely lacked experience. I handled the young

The author leads a pack string through the Rocky Mountains

horses carefully, wanting them to learn things properly and not get accustomed to bad habits. The trip to camp had gone well, with no problems.

Our master plan was the same as the previous year. We would hunt for only one elk. As usual, I dreamed of seeing Mr. Big and promised myself I would not squeeze the trigger on anything less. Time was no concern for us; we had no reason to hurry our hunt. I had a feeling it would be Meredith who would do the shooting that year.

We had a day or two to pass before the season opened. It was enjoyable to take inventory of the trout population in the nearby streams and lakes. The aspen trees had dropped nearly all their golden leaves, but several varieties of low bushes seemed to glow with red and yellow. Several times, we observed small bands of elk. One band was trailed by one of the biggest five-point bulls I had ever seen. More interesting was the fact that nearly every cow was followed by a calf. We figured the elk must have really cooperated with each other during the previous autumn to have produced such a bumper calf crop.

"It appears the critters are doing their best to make sure there are always elk in the mountains," I said to Meredith. "Now, if we humans can show enough wisdom to hold up our end of the deal, these elk will be here from now on."

"That's a big 'if,'" she replied.

An hour's walk from our camp was a ridge overlooking several open parks just below timberline. The surrounding area was an elk haven, full of well-used trails, rubbed trees, and wallows.

Meredith and I reached the ridge on foot at first light on opening morning of elk season. We found an excellent lookout spot and knelt down behind a large fallen tree. We looked, listened, watched, and waited. Nothing moved. Clearly we had were at the right spot at the wrong time.

I glassed a distant, grassy mountain slope just as the sun rose. The slope was nearly two miles away, and on it grazed a herd of elk. Through my spotting scope, I could see a good amount of antler on two bulls. We started for the distant herd, hunting our way as we went.

Perhaps a half-hour later, we found another promising spot and paused to look around. Part of the herd we had spotted was still in view on the grassy slope. Through the spotting scope, I now saw the bulls clearly. Both were better six-pointers than most elk hunters ever see, but they weren't the elk I was looking for. I then turned my attention to two single cows that appeared to be barren and fat.

We watched the elk until they grazed into a small island of timber. The sun had been up for quite a while, and we figured the herd would bed down in the trees for the remainder of the day. When no elk reappeared after another half-hour, we started walking toward the distant island of trees. From two hundred yards away, we stopped to look things over. The small patch of timber was three or four acres and on a steep hillside. We knew the herd was somewhere within the trees but would be tricky to hunt. I moved a few steps for a better view and walked into plain sight of a cow bedded at the bottom of the timber. The heifer laid under a tree and stared at us.

"I don't see a calf with her," I whispered to Meredith. "Take a steady rest and shoot her."

"No," Meredith answered. "She's too far."

Two hundred yards was not an unreasonable distance, but Meredith was uncomfortable with the shot. I was proud of her for having the self control to refuse an unsure shot. She whispered to me as we watched the bedded cow: "You shoot her before she spooks the others."

"No, she's too far for me too," I whispered back.

Meredith gave me a funny look just as the cow got to her feet and trotted away from us without alarming the other elk. The path of her escape gave us an idea. It seemed to be a natural trail to and from the timber patch. Meredith stationed herself about eighty yards from the trail and used a dead limb as a steady rifle rest. I planned to circle the timber and work my way into the trees. If the elk left the trees on the trail Meredith watched, it would be duck soup from her ambush.

I made a wide circle to the top of the patch of trees and discovered four cow elk bedded on a grassy bench seventy-five yards below me. I froze to see what they would do. One cow spotted me, while another looked in the opposite direction. Two of the cows slept with their heads on the ground. The cow watching me looked on with little interest. Finally, after several minutes, I gave a loud whistle, with hopes of arousing the cows without stampeding them. All four cows got to their feet and looked around before slowly disappearing into the trees. The timber concealed more elk than we knew. Suddenly, from three separate routes, elk began filing from the patch of timber. The largest bunch— followed by a six-point bull—slowly marched on the trail near Meredith and stopped, nose to tail, less than a hundred yards from her.

I heard a single, sharp report from Meredith's .257 Roberts and watched the elk trot back into the trees. The other elk stopped and stared over their shoulders. Everything seemed unusually quiet. Then, from behind a small tree above where Meredith knelt, I saw a cow elk roll twice and lay still. The excitement still was not over.

In a moment, a six-point bull and two cows climbed the hill toward me. I froze while they walked to within twenty-five yards of me, where I could literally watch them blink their eyes. Faced in my direction, the handsome bull rubbed a tree with his white-tipped antlers, and bugled loudly. I sat quietly and watched him bugle a second time, his calls ringing the silence. Then, suddenly, I had an urge to show myself. The bull looked surprised, but did not run when I stood. It seemed he knew I was not a danger to him. We looked at each other for a short time before I turned and walked away.

"We have what we came for, and now we'll leave you be," I said to the bull. He watched as I descended the hill to Meredith.

We saw no elk the following day, as we packed the quartered elk to camp. Before leaving the kill site, I again examined the large hole that Meredith's bullet had put through the cow's heart.

"That was good shooting, honey," I told her.

"I was aiming for the head," she shot back at me.

"Oh."

Our spirits were light as we moved through the beautiful forest. It was a carefree, blue-sky day—the kind of day when the world seemed right and life made sense. It was a good day just to be alive.

We relaxed around camp for the next few days, as a storm left a few inches of light snow. We kept hot drinks on the tin stove while we boned the elk quarters to lighten the load. We packed the bones a few miles from camp. A couple of days later, we checked them as we left the mountains and, as we had predicted, a black bear had cleaned up the pile.

The trip out took two days. A drizzling rain fell on our overnight camp. Just as we finished packing the horses the next morning, huge thick, heavy flakes of snow began gently falling from the gray clouds overhead. Soon the world was white, and I felt a wonderful contentment as the horses moved down the trail.

Chapter Two
Colorado Roots

 I can still remember fairly well the first time I went big-game hunting. We were looking for mule deer somewhere near the South Park in Colorado. My father led while the four of us kids trotted along behind, trying to be as silent as possible. I was the fourth of six children, and on that day finally old enough to be allowed to fall in line behind my older brothers and sister as we tagged along with Dad during his fall hunting.

We were young, wild-eyed and excited; we did not know what to expect but took our cues from Dad and each other. Dad once turned to us, pointed to a pine limb stripped of bark, and whispered, "porcupine." Number-one child seriously turned to number two, pointed and whispered, "porcupine." Number two, in turn, gave number three the whispered "porcupine," and number three related the woodcraft lesson to me.

I just nodded my head to the other three to show that by then I had received the message about the fact that porcupines chewed on trees. Pleased with ourselves that we were worthy students of nature, the four of us whirled and hurried off to catch up with Dad. A script writer for some of those yesteryear TV comedy shows like "The Little Rascals" and "The Three Stooges" could have collected some great material by following Papa Duck and his four ducklings as we stalked the forest for deer that day.

I recall that the five of us stopped by a stock tank half-filled with water, and another lesson of nature was presented, though the significance of it did not register with me for a good number of years. A squirrel had fallen into the tank. I did not know if it had slipped while trying to get a drink or had jumped in by mistake, but the result was the same: death by drowning. We removed the squirrel in order to keep the water from becoming contaminated, though the cattle that drank there probably would not have cared if the water tasted a little like decomposed squirrel.

The lesson? Simply that man's actions have an effect on wildlife and environment—a lesson too complex and deep to be understood by a knee-high curtain climber like I was at the time, but a concept I often consider now.

It was during this same hunt that I first saw an animal fall to a hunter's bullet. The five of us had stopped at the edge of a good-sized grassy park and peered at the opening from behind the bordering trees. A rifle shot a half-mile away caused all heads to spin in the direction from which it had come. More to himself than to us, Dad whispered, "shot," and, of course, the message was dominoed down to me in the usual manner.

Suddenly, a small bunch of does and fawns, followed by a small buck, burst from the opposite side of the park and bounded straight toward us. Dad ordered us to move back into the trees a short distance and stay still; then he dropped down on one knee and steadied his rifle against the trunk of a tree. We kids ran for cover as if a herd of grizzlies was thundering down on us. Dad was more or less concealed by his tree rest. What probably caused the deer to stop seventy five yards away was the sight of four little wild-eyed heads stuck from behind the towering pines.

The deer may have mistaken us for some sort of strange-looking owls. They froze and stared at us, and we froze and stared hard at them for what seemed like hours. I did not have enough sense to see that the small buck Dad wanted was behind a doe. Impatience and inexperience got the best of me, and I moved to ask my oldest brother in a fairly loud voice, "Why doesn't Dad shoot?"

Of course, the deer spooked and bounded away with the buck still shielded by does. Dad decided a doe was as good to eat as any buck and a lot better than nothing. "BOOM!" went his rifle and down went a doe. Dad never scolded me for speaking at the wrong time, but my brothers and sister let me know I had made a mistake. I received a good education that day.

I learned a lot as I examined the dead doe. I was fascinated by her large ears, designed for better hearing. I noted how her hair was different from that of our family dog's. Later, when she was skinned, I inspected, marveled at, and finally realized the holes on each side of her rib cage were actually bullet holes from Dad's rifle. I was spellbound.

Many questions popped into my mind. Why was the hole in the barrel of the rifle so small compared to the holes in the deer? How did the bullet travel from the rifle to the deer? At that age, I didn't really grasp the concept of velocities caused by explosions and of mushrooming bullets. Later, at home, I started with the basics, and it was my mother who explained how a rifle killed a deer.

Using an empty drinking glass to represent a cartridge, she patiently explained how primers, when struck, ignited the powder which sent a bullet through a rifle barrel at high speed. So that was it! I discarded my theory that when the trigger was pulled, the rifle would boom like a cap gun and that it was God himself who then checked to see if the rifle sights were indeed aimed exactly at the deer. If so, he would smite the animal.

Of course, I see the truth of things more clearly these days. I know very well that it is not God who looks down the barrel, but nasty demons instead who sometimes jinx the bullet and cause it to curve in the most mysterious manner. How else can I explain missing a young, fat buck standing broadside at eighty yards last fall?

The next time my father went hunting, I begged to go along and, in fact, slept with my hunting clothes on the night before we left.

❦

Forty-five miles an hour was about the top speed of the three-speed Willys Jeep, and the one hundred and twenty miles to the mountain cabin seemed to drag on forever. Conversation was difficult because of the roaring motor, but the Jeep had a great heater, which Dad and I were glad to have. It was October—the last week of hunting season—and a blizzard had just swept through the Colorado Rockies. As the Jeep labored through the cold air that Friday afternoon, my mind and spirit were already at the cabin.

The cabin belonged to Dean Hardgrove, my father's long-time friend and hunting partner. Dean bought the ghost-town cabin more than fifteen years earlier, and with his wife and others had renovated it into a comfortable high-country hideaway. Dean was much more to me than just my father's friend. He was something like a favorite uncle and had a profound effect on my early years. This kind, humorous man influenced my outdoor education more than any other person. I was lucky to have him for my mentor. Dad was not Dean's only hunting partner, so it was very unusual that only Dad and I were using the cabin at that time of year.

Not only did we have the cabin to ourselves, but we also had a monopoly on the surrounding mountains. We didn't see a single other person that weekend. I suffered from the usual restless night-before-the-hunt syndrome. One of the symptoms was closing my eyes and seeing visions of huge-antlered bucks moving through buck-brush basins near timberline. Long before morning, we left the cabin and drove the Jeep along a rough road built by gold miners for their horses and wagons many years before.

The ground was covered by a foot of fresh, sparking snow, and I wondered if the deer and elk had already migrated to lower elevations. My question was answered by the animal tracks criss-crossing a snowy opening near timberline. Dad stopped the Jeep, and we got out to look around and consider any likely areas to hunt on foot. I had barely stepped from the vehicle and was turning from it when a movement some one hundred and seventy five yards away caught my eye.

My heart instantly started to hammer. At that point in my hunting career, I had shot small game, a deer and an antelope. Yet I was not prepared for the sight of three tremendous buck mule deer as they slowly walked away from us.

To put it mildly, I fell to pieces. The bucks stopped and looked back while I, with shaking hands, somehow chambered a cartridge.

I knelt in the snow and whispered to Dad: "The biggest one is behind the tree in front of the other two."

Dad never even made an effort to get his rifle from the Jeep, and only now after many years can I understand why. He saw the deer; he saw his young son, rifle in hand, ready to shoot. He decided it was my hunt, my moment, and he only wished to watch.

In effect, Dad was giving me a chance to prove what kind of hunter I was. I failed miserably. The biggest buck stepped from behind the small tree. I found him in my rifle scope and sent a bullet on its way. The three bucks bounced and trotted away while I continued to blast away without results. I'm not sure how many times I reloaded the four-shot magazine but I suddenly realized I was running out of ammunition. Only then did I collect myself enough to really concentrate on putting a bullet into the big buck.

The deer stopped broadside about four hundred yards away near the edge of thick timber. Knowing it was then or never, I sprawled flat in the snow with that marvelous buck staring at me as I steadied the crosshairs and slowly squeezed the trigger. The rifle boomed and bucked once again. The buck gave a mighty leap and disappeared into the timber. I somehow knew that my last shot had also missed, and I continued to lie in the snow as an angry, empty feeling grew within me. The silence of the mountains returned, then grew unbearable.

Finally, I arose to follow the deer's trail through the snow to check for blood. At the place where I had fired my last shot, I could plainly see the path of the bullet as it had skimmed the surface of the snow. I had not allowed for enough drop and had shot six inches below the buck's heart. Bucks, like fish that get away, never grow smaller with the passing of time, but I am still convinced that buck fever prevented me from having my name printed in the record book at the age of fifteen.

Three good things happened during and after that hunt. Most important, I did not wound the buck. Secondly, I checked very carefully for blood. The final thing was the advice that Dean Hardgrove gave me a week later when I told him the story.

Elk season opened the following weekend, and a fair-sized group of hunters was headquartered at Dean's cabin. Among them were Dean, Dad, two of my brothers, and me. What a hunting camp we had! One must realize that, to our group of serious and dedicated hunters, elk were the ultimate big game. Once a year, we would do enough planning and work to be the envy of any military operation in the world. We brought in food by the box load, checked our four-wheel-drive vehicles, stacked wood to the porch rafters, gave our boots a final waterproofing treatment, scrutinized maps, fed and watered pack animals, honed our knives repeatedly, and discussed our strategies. Of course, everything and everybody naturally revolved around Dean and his stories.

Dean's talent for storytelling was nearly mystical; just listening to him was half the pleasure of every hunt we shared. In his younger days, Dean had been everywhere, done everything, and was always known to call a spade a spade. Yet never did I hear him talk meanly about anyone.

One of the stories Dean told us was about a large herd of elk he and Dad had followed through the snow and timber for several days. They were so close behind the phantom herd that the elk's droppings still steamed, yet they never even caught sight of the animals. Stories like that convinced me that to shoot a bull elk would be one of the highest achievements of my life, and I hoped that if the opportunity ever came, I would not repeat my dismal previous performance.

The opportunity came on Saturday afternoon. We had all been eager to be in our favorite spots in the surrounding elk country on opening morning. Some of us left the cabin on foot while others headed out in four-wheel drives. My oldest brother's chosen area was on a long ridge just above timberline. Flanked by two small streams and covered with buck-brush, it was a perfect spot for elk. Because the ridge was the farthest from the cabin and required miles of uphill walking, my brother got up and started out several hours before the rest.

Dean, Dad, and I drove with a few others to a different area and set out on foot to work some timber and grassy parks. It was a pleasant morning— blue sky above white peaks—but it produced no elk for our group of hunters.

Dean and I returned to the vehicles ahead of the others and visited while we waited. During our conversation, I told him about missing the big buck deer, and he gave me advice that I will keep forever. His words were actually obvious to a hunter but his magical method of talking branded them into my brain like a hot iron. From the way his eyes danced and the constant faint smile on his weathered face, I saw that he read me like a book. He placed a work-worn, callused hand on my knee and said softly: "Don't squeeze the trigger unless the crosshairs are on the animal."

Simple enough words, but spoken in a manner and spirit that would make them echo through my head late that very afternoon as I centered the crosshairs of my scope on a beautiful bull elk.

Our group had returned to the cabin and was discussing plans for the afternoon while eating lunch. Suddenly my oldest brother returned from his hunt on the ridge, panting more from excitement than from his walk. Too far for a rifle shot, he had watched forty head of elk climb out of the drainage he was in and move through a high, snow-filled pass. The herd bull had antlers that nearly reached to his rump when he laid his head back to watch the rest of the herd climb the steep hillside above him.

We calculated where the herd was headed and decided if we hurried, we could hunt them that afternoon. The cabin turned into instant chaos. We sorted and gathered gear in a fashion that resembled a pie-eating contest and a square dance taking place simultaneously on a department-store escalator. Somehow, we got lined out and on the way. My two older brothers and I volunteered to walk into the hunting area from a roadless route, while the rest of our group tried other locations.

My brothers and I spaced ourselves a few hundred yards apart and slowly worked up the side of a heavily timbered mountain, with plans to meet above timberline. Two hours later, I eased out of the last of the trees and stood at the bottom of a steep hillside covered with buck-brush and small patches of wind-stunted trees.

The sight of two cow elk staring at me from one hundred and fifty yards away startled me, and I quickly knelt with my rifle ready. The cows then looked away from me to one of the patches of short trees. From the trees slowly walked a medium-sized bull elk. I, of course, fell to pieces, put the bull in my scope, and snapped off a round. The bull was untouched and stopped after three leaps to stare at me and then at the cows.

With shaking hands, I chambered another cartridge and threw the rifle to my shoulder. That's when it happened. Dean's words—"Don't squeeze the trigger unless the crosshairs are on the animal"—came to me so plainly that I expected to turn around and see him standing behind me. I paused, collected myself, put the crosshairs on the bull's chest, and gently squeezed the trigger. The rifle boomed and kicked. In slow motion, the bull reared on his hind legs, fell completely over backward, then crashed and rolled to the bottom of the hill.

❦

My annual schedule as a teen-ager remained pretty much the same from year to year. School burned up the bulk of my time. Summer found me at my grandparents' ranch, where I helped raise cattle and wheat. The few weeks before school started in the fall were, however, reserved for time in the mountains. That was the best time of the year. I was young and carefree; the mountains were wild, interesting, and challenging. It was within the embrace of that sweet country that I defined freedom.

Sometimes with a friend or brother along, but often alone and on foot, I would roam the Colorado highcountry. No trail was left unexplored, no fishing hole was left untried and—after I took up bow hunting—no basin was left unchecked.

At that time, bow season for deer and elk opened on the same day. We always hunted for both species, but mainly concentrated on deer because they were more numerous. We thought it best to save our energy for elk until rifle season, but the primary reason was that our favorite basin seldom attracted elk. The basin's main attraction for us was that the large majority of deer in it were always bucks—big bucks. After making that discovery, the basin was normally our chosen spot on opening morning of bow season.

I am certain a purist bow hunter would have been appalled at our group. We were competent shots, but our tactics and style definitely lacked refinement. Among us, camouflage was virtually nonexistent. Making a tree stand or blind was not for us. We could not tolerate being motionless for longer than a few minutes. More than once, I stalked close enough for a reasonable bow shot and then just watched until the animal moved away because I wanted only to study game up close. Hunting was merely an excuse to be in the highcountry and, even though shooting a deer or an elk was our goal, we never felt disappointed if we did not kill one. From our point of view, it was more fun to see how close we could stalk an animal before it spooked than to merely stalk close enough for a shot. Because of this modest goal, we were never let down. Every hunt was a success.

The only elk I ever shot with a bow was after a long stalk with perfect conditions. I was hunting alone and walked to the hunting area leading a packhorse. I found a nice camp at timberline with plenty of feed, water, and wood. My packhorse was the only horse I have ever known that would stay around camp without hobbles or a picket rope. At night, she voluntarily stood next to my small tent like a faithful dog. I could hear her shift her weight from leg to leg, and, just before daylight, I would be awakened as she moved off to graze nearby. What a joy she was!

I had walked out of camp after first light on a beautiful day and moved slowly along a well-used game trail in heavy timber. Step, stop, look, listen. During one of my stops, I saw something move ahead of me. I carefully got into shooting position. A doe and two fuzzy, spotted fawns walked to within twenty feet of me before the doe, perhaps suspecting my presence, froze. She sniffed the air while looking everywhere. After a short time, she shook her black-tipped tail and left the game trail to continue on her way. The three deer moved in absolute silence.

I happily returned to camp with thoughts of breakfast on my mind. From my campfire, I watched a small band of cow and calf elk as they moved across the hillside above me. Then I saw another single animal on the hillside, grazing slowly among the buck-brush. It appeared reddish and about the size of a deer. I thought the chances were good it was a lone buck and finished my coffee while waiting for the animal to lie down for a mid-morning snooze. After it did, I memorized the hillside, determined my best route of approach, and started the steep climb. The key to that stalk was the wind, which continued steadily from the same direction and was strong enough to muffle little noises. After about forty-five minutes, I was within forty yards of the bush where the animal had bedded, but I still had not seen it.

I took off my light boots, and, wearing only heavy wool socks on my feet, slowly started toward the bush from slightly above it. At fifteen yards, I finally saw a reddish patch of hair. The animal's head was down, and I still could not tell what it was. I eased forward again. When I was ten yards directly above the animal, it finally raised its head—a calf elk! I did not wish to shoot the four-month-old calf, but decided to see how close I could get before it sensed me. I had always wanted to stalk an animal close enough so that I could touch it with an arrow. This seemed like a perfect opportunity.

The rest of the stalk may have lasted ten minutes or two hours, I don't really know. At one point, the calf turned its head in my direction and I thought the jig was up, but it soon turned away and continued watching below. I was about six feet away and close enough to touch the calf with my bow. I wondered why the young elk did not hear my heartbeat. That was when it stood up. The calf awkwardly stretched and made a puddle of water under it—a bull calf. Then I saw why it was by itself without a cow nearby. Its front leg was broken below the knee, causing the hoof to stick out at nearly a ninety-degree angle. The calf could not keep up and would probably die during the coming winter.

I considered the fate of the crippled calf and slowly drew my bow. The few seconds it took for the calf to die seemed like an easier fate than the one destined for a later time. After a while, I descended the hill to camp and saddled my packhorse to retrieve the elk.

That hunt was one of the few stalks I have made in which everything went according to plan. There have been dozens of unsuccessful, yet interesting and enjoyable stalks. I still chuckle when I think of one hunt that was perfect until the instant I released my arrow.

I was bow hunting late in the afternoon and slowly gumshoed through the trees at timberline. Bull elk bugled occasionally but not in my immediate area. The grass was deep, lush, and damp from a recent rain. I frequently checked the breeze to make sure it continued to drift into my face. Something flickered a hundred yards ahead and caused me to freeze instantly. It was the ear of a forked-horn deer. I slowly sidestepped two paces to conceal myself behind a tree. As I watched and waited, a second buck appeared. Both were rolling-fat forked-horns, "pan-sized" bucks. Quietly, they grazed directly toward me, taking care to pick only the tastiest tidbits from the mountainside smorgasbord.

I knelt into shooting position and watched their approach through the limbs of the small tree. The tree was too tall to shoot over from my crouched position. I faced the downhill side of the tree, which proved to be an error. The first buck to graze into a spot where I could shoot happened to pass the tree on the uphill side, forcing me to swing the bow almost ninety degrees to my left. My left hand, holding the bow, now was nearly straight out to my side instead of in front of me. The range was less than twenty feet. Needless to say, my movements were very slow and deliberate.

I waited until the buck looked directly away from me, then aimed and released the arrow. I felt a sudden strong tug on my right-hand vest pocket and, unbelievingly, watched my arrow stick weakly into the dirt ten feet in front of me, as if I had thrown it by hand. The two deer bounced away while I tried to figure out what had happened. It was my custom to carry a small flashlight in the pocket of my down vest. After being released, the bowstring had snagged the bulge in my vest.

The bucks never did determine what had spooked them and came back to investigate. They snorted occasionally and walked with stiff legs, their necks jerking like a birds. Again, I froze behind the small tree until they approached within bow range. Then, with a laugh, I arose and told them to get the heck out of there.

Though we rarely killed anything, the adventure of bow hunting was interesting and rewarding enough to make us try it each fall for many years. We normally hunted twice each day, at daylight and again from late afternoon until last light. We always left camp with the same enthusiasm and excitement, never quite sure what sights the next few hours held in store.

One of the main differences I noticed between bow and rifle hunting was how little the game reacted to bow hunting. It seemed that after the first few shots of rifle season, game was unpredictably dispersed and overly wary, even when not spooked. My bow-hunting experiences were much different.

Often we camped relatively close to our hunting area, making no great effort to conceal our location, noise, or smoke. We did not exactly march around smudge fires beating on brass drums, but neither did we tiptoe around camp eating cold soup. We merely made ourselves at home in the woods as any camper would. Probably the loudest disturbance was our excited shouting from the trout stream. We often hunted the same routes and places, yet rarely did we fail to see game.

Surprisingly, we often saw the same individual animals. We became so familiar with some deer and elk that we named them. Big Red and The Caribou were trophy-sized deer, while several elk were described with less romantic labels, such as "the spike with funny horns" or "the blue neck-band cow." That particular cow was seen a number of times one fall, and she seemed always to be the lookout for a small band of elk. Invariably, she was the one that would spot us and alert the others. Soon we called her "the barking blue neck-band cow," and later that fall she became "the loud-mouthed barking blue neck-band cow."

I have many treasured memories of the mountains during fall bow-hunting trips, but two scenes always stand out in my mind. One is the sight of a handsome six-point bull elk bugling time and time again as I watched from forty yards away. The second is of twelve buck mule deer, still in velvet, standing head to tail on a steep rockslide. One buck was a fork-horn, and the other eleven all had four points or more to a side. Several were heavy-beamed, long-tined record-book candidates. Such a sight I will never see again. These animals are my mental trophies, stored in an honored spot in my mind and as sacred as any head mount on any wall. They are riches I will treasure until my dying hour.

❦

The sad part of many endeavors is that by the time a person finally figures things out and gets the hang of it, they have to move on to something else. So it was with me and my hunts in the Colorado highcountry. Gradually through those years, I had demystified elk from nearly mythological beasts to something closer to reality. I realized they were beautiful animals with keen senses and predictable behavior. Just when I got to the point where I could routinely see and often shoot elk, I moved away from Colorado and my beloved boreal hunting grounds. A half-dozen years elapsed before I was able to return and participate in a grand and very special elk hunt.

That particular homecoming was one of the most enjoyable I have ever known, and it was special for many reasons. It was a rendezvous and rediscovery of common interests for my father and me. We were in a familiar place, away from the hustle and bustle of the city, where we again had the opportunity to enjoy each other's company. The mountains have an uncanny ability to remove all pretense, clear away all shams, and expose all merits and shortcomings.

During that hunt, Dad and I reinforced our father-son bond. Another factor that made it a special hunt was my nephew, a lad in his early teens who was glad to have the excuse of hunting in order to miss a day of school. Through his eyes, I watched the entire hunt and recalled my own teen-age adventures. The fourth person in the group was, perhaps, the main reason the hunt was so special. That person was my wife, who, for the first time, saw all the wonderful and magnificent scenes I had so often recalled for her.

Our destination was Dean Hardgrove's cabin. He and his wife had moved to Arizona a few years before, and we learned before we left to go hunting that Dean had been taken to an Arizona hospital because of a very serious illness. Yet, numerous times during that weekend elk hunt I keenly sensed his presence and expected to see him walk through the cabin doorway at any moment. He had figured out a way to join us in spirit, if not in the flesh.

Because we would be staying at the cabin—where we had beds, stoves, cooking utensils and (dare I say it?) electric lights—we didn't need a huge amount camping gear. Some of my fellow guides and elk hunters may scoff at the idea of having such luxuries anywhere within twenty miles of an elk camp, and I can well understand their line of reasoning. When I think about the dozens of times I have gone hunting in the wilderness with little more than a bedroll and frying pan, though, I reserve to right to pamper myself now and again.

I serviced the station wagon we used to pull the horse trailer, and inspected the tire chains. I tested the trailer's lights and greased the wheel bearings before hooking it to the car. It had always been Dad's custom to take charge of food organizing and cooking on all of our hunting and fishing trips. This was fortunate for us because Dad had an appreciation for good food and had never been known to cut any culinary corners.

We made our escape from the city early Friday, with the idea of going on a combination firewood gathering and sightseeing trip that afternoon. We finally packed the gear into the sagging station wagon, lashed a few hay bales to the overhead luggage rack, and headed for the highcountry. Dad was exhausted from working overtime at his office in order to have a three-day weekend and was delighted when I volunteered to drive. This gave him the opportunity to nap, and we had barely passed the city limits before he was sound asleep.

I made no effort to conceal my eagerness to explore my old hunting grounds once again. I was anxious to see if the mountains were indeed as magnificent as I remembered them. To my delight, they were. At about noon, we turned off the main highway and ascended a scenic road flanked on each side by towering peaks more than 14,000 feet in elevation. We were soon in valleys of golden-aspen hillsides, silent stands of spruce and lodgepole, and icy streams. When I first caught sight of the cabin, it was like seeing an old friend. As I stepped from the station wagon, the surrounding giant peaks seemed to look down and say, "Welcome back."

I looked up, smiled, and replied aloud, "It's good to be here," then hurried to unload the horse and mule from the trailer. Soon after, we settled into the cabin and devoted the afternoon to gathering wood, relaxing, taking in the sights, and making final preparations for the following morning's elk hunt.

It was interesting to note some of the slight changes of usual roles during that hunt. My wife took charge of the cooking department, while Dad settled into a rocking chair and, unknowingly, assumed Dean's position as storyteller and camp overseer. My nephew acted as I had at his age. He explored up and down the creek, behind the cabin, and across the valley. He soon knew every tree, rock, and path. My contribution was looking after the pack animals and figuring out the best spot to be at daylight on Saturday, the first day of elk season.

In order to reach our chosen spot by daylight, we left the cabin on foot at 4 a.m. and hiked up a trail that led to elk country. It was a beautiful night, moonless, windless, with thousands of bright stars twinkling like diamonds. I brought up the rear and held a flashlight on the other's feet so we could all find our way in the darkness. My wife had hiked the Pacific Crest Trail from California to Washington, my nephew was a cross-country runner, and I was known to hold my own with any group of walkers. We let desk-bound Dad lead the way and set a pace that suited him. I chuckled as I remembered how my brothers and I used to practically trot in breathless awe at Dad's ground-gaining walk. Now it was he who panted during the frequent stops.

There was only one elk license and one rifle among us, and both belonged to Dad. Fairly early in our morning hike, we persuaded him to let us take turns packing the rifle until we reached the hunting area. This chore was done, for the most part, by my wife and nephew because I was hampered by a backpack full of lunch, extra clothing, rope, and other gear.

Our timing was perfect, and we arrived at the edge of the hunting area just at the first sign of dawn. We paused near an ancient, decaying cabin beside a collapsed gold mine. I wanted to show my wife the old, abandoned cabin where I had often stayed and shared the floor with pack rats, shoeshoe rabbits, porcupines, and other citizens of the forest. As we entered the rotten structure, she made some remark about how varmints stuck together.

Just then, a bull elk bugled nearby—close enough to make us freeze and drop our voices to whispers. We slowly retreated behind some timber to allow the sky to brighten enough for shooting. The bull bugled several more times from beyond a small hill a quarter of a mile above us.

After what seemed like hours, we agreed there was enough light to shoot and eased toward the hill. Slowly topping the crest, we initially saw nothing in the meadow on the other side. The bull had stopped bugling and gave us no clue to his location. Suddenly, we saw the first elk of the day. Far above us, more than a mile away, six elk ran like race horses across a mountain slope. We guessed other hunters had entered the drainage from the other direction and had spooked the elk. A few minutes later, two hunters walked quickly across the mountain slope, following the elk. Those were the only hunters we saw that day.

At that point, we made a mistake. We had given up hope of seeing the bull that bugled at daylight, and the four of us had come together in a huddle at the edge of the meadow to discuss our next move. From the timbered hillside above the meadow, two cow elk stepped into view and walked down a rocky clearing toward us. They saw us just as we saw them. We all froze and stared at each other from two hundred yards apart. We had been caught flat-footed. In a moment, the cows slowly turned and faded back into the timber. I quickly glassed the timber with my binoculars and confirmed what I had suspected—a movement of yellow hair, a glimpse of antler, and the bull also vanished.

Again we huddled to make plans. I proposed we hotfoot to the head of a nearby small creek that was a central crossing place and feeding area for elk in that area. I reasoned that because there were elk and other hunters moving in the area, the small basin at the head of the creek might be a good place to see an elk. Dad had nearly played himself out from the morning walk, but was game to try. I was the only one among us who had ever been to the basin, so I led the way up the creek. I deliberately slowed the pace and stopped often to let Dad catch his breath.

In addition to the thin air, I figured one mistake for the day was enough and didn't want to charge recklessly into a bunch of elk. At timberline, we beheld a spectacular sight. We had paused behind a small bunch of trees to study the basin. Movement and the deep, heavy bugle of a big bull drew our attention to the tall brush a half-mile above us. Through my binoculars I could see elk moving everywhere, and once saw the white-tipped points of a big bull as they rocked through the brush. Again the bull bugled and was answered by a small bull. Dad put his binoculars down and was unable to conceal the excitement in his voice: "That whole hillside is moving!"

Indeed it was moving—and rapidly—toward us. It appeared that a band of elk with a small bull had been spooked into the basin and had unintentionally run into the herd with the big, and now very upset, bull. The herds joined and were nervously working their way down to timberline when we spotted them. We lost sight of them as we quickly shifted our position in order to cover their probable routes.

One route was along the small creek bottom, one hundred yards to our right, and the second was along timberline, fifty yards in front of us. The herds were somewhere behind a small strip of trees eighty yards ahead. We waited breathlessly for the elk to appear. For too long, we waited and waited. No bugles, no movement—something was wrong. Had the elk smelled or heard us? Were they standing motionless just out of our view? Were the herds moving away? Somehow the elk must have sensed us but not pinpointed our location.

Suddenly, a long file of elk came into view on a steep, bare hillside a hundred and seventy five yards away. Cows, spike, more cows, then a small bull. The bull made the fatal mistake of stopping broadside and looking back down the slope. At that instant, Dad's rifle spoke once, and the bull's neck was broken by the bullet. We watched the dead bull roll down the steep hillside and then lost sight of him as he tumbled behind the strip of trees. Evidently, the dead bull must have rolled into the big bull on his way down the slope. As the tumbling elk disappeared from sight, the big bull suddenly came leaping into view. He stopped on the hillside and stared down at his now-defunct antagonist with disbelief and amazement. We supposed the big bull had never been charged in such an unorthodox style. He regained his composure and ambled up the slope, following the other elk.

Then the work began. Because it was still early in the day, we had enough time to pack the elk to the cabin, if we hurried. My wife and nephew were dispatched to the cabin to saddle the pack animals and return with them. Dad and I stayed to dress and quarter the bull. We soon finished our task and ate our lunch. Dad found a sunny spot at the bottom of a nearby tree and made himself comfortable for a well-earned nap. I climbed a short distance up the hill to find a better spot to look over the surrounding scenery.

With great contentment, I sat and reflected upon all the things those mountains were to me. I was thankful for all the adventures and experiences that had taken place beneath their tall peaks. A more sobering thought formed in my mind as I considered the future of the mountains: I could not help wondering if my family would have the opportunity to participate in a good hunt such as I had, and if there would be enough remaining habitat to hunt elk in another ten or twenty years.

My mountain meditation was suddenly interrupted as my wife and nephew came into sight below me. I was surprised to see they had returned with the pack animals so quickly. They were riding the animals, which partly explained their fast time. An involuntary groan left me as I thought about the two of them perched on the sawbuck pack saddles. I had ridden on a pack saddle a time or two and was convinced it was the most uncomfortable way ever devised to ride a horse.

We mantied the quartered elk, then packed it on the animals. A dark, gray sky warned of approaching snow as we started off the mountain. I chose to lead the packed mule myself because she showed signs of disapproval at having to carry half an elk. She dearly wanted to shed her load during the entire trip to the cabin, but I successfully persuaded her otherwise.

With the mule trying to run, turn around, buck, roll, and stampede, I set a fast pace downhill. My wife led the well-broke, docile pack mare. My nephew decided to take a shortcut straight down the mountain instead of following the trail, but became rim-rocked and arrived at the cabin an hour after the rest of us. Dear ol' Dad had put in a long day and was completely exhausted by the time he reached the cabin.

There, we quickly took care of the pack animals and finished all the necessary camp chores. My nephew grabbed a bar of soap and towel and headed for a partly iced-over beaver pond to freshen up. I declined his invitation to go along and told him that if I jumped in that water, I would jump out so fast I wouldn't even get wet.

My wife, Dad, and I felt the effects of our hike and soon were shuffling around the cabin floor. Hot food revitalized us and again gave us a rosy outlook on life. That night, I could not picture a more perfect or contented hunting camp: My wife finished the kitchen chores and waited to take on the winner of the cribbage game my nephew and I were playing; Dad relaxed in a rocking chair and talked of past hunts he had taken with Dean; and outside the cabin, the pack animals filled themselves with hay and water. The smoke from the fireplace mingled with snow, and a set of elk antlers hung on the porch rafters —an added bonus to a very successful and very special elk hunt.

Snow was still falling the next morning and was piling up rapidly on the ten inches that had accumulated during the night. Dad returned from shoveling a path to the outhouse and remarked how grateful he was that we had not waited a day to pack in the elk. The packhorse and mule looked particularly miserable with a layer of wet snow covering their humped backs.

The thought of traveling snowy mountain roads in a two-wheel-drive vehicle made me wish I was already home. We quickly packed and made sure the cabin was in order before we left the mountains.

As we approached home several hours later, Dad told us he was going to write a long letter to Dean and tell him about our hunt. I thought it was a great idea, but Dad never got a chance to write that letter.

I was eating breakfast Monday morning when we received a phone call I will never forget: Dean—husband, father, friend, teacher, sportsman—had passed away. I suddenly felt a thousand years old and rested my forehead in my hands over my plate. I thought about the timing of events of the weekend elk hunt and wondered if it was only coincidence that Dean had died the night we had returned. How many hundreds of times had he made sure everyone was safely back from hunting before he could put his mind at ease?

It is rare for me to go to the mountains without, at some time, thinking of Dean. I look at a snow-covered peak and see his wrinkled, smiling face; I hear his chuckle in a small creek; I smell his pipe tobacco in my campfire. Dean and Dad had a unique friendship in that they enjoyed sharing their hunting knowledge and experiences with their children as well as with each other. A tradition of education and fun surrounded each fall we spent in the Colorado Rockies. My writing is dedicated to their honor.

Chapter Three
Playing Cat and Mouse with a Granddaddy Bull

 What was the toughest elk hunt I was ever on? That's easy to answer. It was during the fall of 1988. Meredith and I were working for an outfitter in northwest Wyoming. She had hired on as horse wrangler, and I worked as a guide. It was a good camp, well organized and comfortable. The horses carried us the entire season through elk country second to none. The camp cook—who can either make or break any hunting camp—was considered by all to be the best in the West. We killed many bulls that season; it was a success by any elk hunter's measure.

So, what was the tough hunt all about? It was caused by a small band of jittery elk with one old bull, a smart bull who seemed to know what hunters were all about. Perhaps the bull's knowledge was painfully gained from the scar-encased bullet he carried next to the femur bone in one of his hindquarters.

It was about ten days into the season, and there had been enough hunter activity in the area to make the herds wary and elusive. The elk stayed more and more in deep timber, and their nervousness increased. Most of the easy bulls had already made a journey to town on the back of a pack horse. I was guiding Bill from Kansas and his long-time friend and hunting partner, Bill ...from Kansas. In order to avoid confusion with their common names, we soon started referring to one of them as Lars. The other Bill feigned puzzlement by our action and kept insisting that there should be no confusion since he was by far the better looking of the two. Lars confided aloud to all in camp that the other Bill could easily be recognized by his advanced senility.

Regardless of their evaluations of each other, it was clear to me that both were sincere, experienced sportsmen. Both men had previously hunted in Wyoming. Lars had been thrown a kiss by the Greek hunting goddess, Diana, in the form of a huge non-typical mule deer buck. The other Bill had put another leg under a grand slam with a Wyoming bighorn ram. On the first day of hunting, hours before the morning sun even hinted where the eastern horizon lay, Lars, Bill and I crawled onto our ponies and started for elk country. Such midnight rides can amount to something akin to a nocturnal fox hunt in a jungle.

31

This cautious, smart bull finally gave the author and his hunter an opportunity after a nerve-racking wait.

The ride through the moonless, overcast night and up the side of a steep mountain was an interesting experience for us. Just at daylight, we tied our sweat-covered, frosted horses to a group of stunted trees on a wide ridge. The grassy ridge was well sprinkled with white bark pine, providing excellent cover for any animal. We continued to speak in whispers as we walked from the horses.

A fresh dusting of soft snowflakes muffled our footsteps, a slight breeze burned my right cheek. The low, gray sky, soaked up all surrounding noises until even the sound of our breathing seemed greatly amplified. Up to that point, we had not seen nor heard any hint of elk. Even so, the air was charged with an electric suspense. When we were just a hundred yards from our horses, I ventured a bugle into the silence of the misty morning.

Immediately from the scattered trees ahead came a strange-sounding, half-hearted response from a bull. Until then, the hunt had been easy, a textbook search for elk. The thirty minutes from the time we heard the brief responding bugle until we saw the bull was the most intense, toughest, nip-and-tuck elk hunt I ever experienced. During those nerve-racking minutes, we pushed our strained senses to their limits while stalking unseen elk with the odds in their favor. Perhaps more important than our eyes and ears was an inexplicable intuition that came into play. Some gut feeling helped us as we played a winner-take-all game of cat and mouse.

After hearing the single response, I ventured another bugle. No reply. After a few minutes, I again tried to make the bull respond and give us an advantage. Again nothing. Knowing little more than that there was at least one bull somewhere ahead, we began easing in the direction from where the bull bugled. No 1960s Vietnam patrol ever moved with as much caution and tension as we moved. In a short distance, we crouched beneath low limbs of a tree and peeked to the scattered timber in front of us. From under low branches, we watched the legs of an elk move slowly out of sight as if the animal was feeding. Then, suddenly, the yellow and black rump of a second elk faded away.

We then knew that there were at least two elk and that they did not seem alarmed. Believing the bull we had heard earlier was near, I waited for a moment and again tried a bugle. Once again, no response. This often is a sign of a spooked bull.

We waited for a short time before again creeping ahead. Perhaps after a hundred yards—and what seemed a hundred years—we saw a few fresh tracks in the dusting of snow. The tracks intertwined through the small trees, clearly showing that the elk were restless and not eager to leave the protection of the scattered trees.

Once more I bugled and once more not a sound came back. The silence was eerie. I decided to stop bugling. It was evident that the bull, if he was still near, simply was not interested in telling us where he was. I understood too well that excessive bugling at such a bull is foolish.

We inched ahead again and came to a lengthy opening along a draw. Lars, Bill and I reached the upper reaches of the opening just in time to see three partially concealed elk move through the thin trees at the bottom of the opening.

The elk were very alert and walked cautiously and deliberately through the protection of available cover. I began to wonder if we followed some sort of phantom elk, floating apparitions that gave us only glimpses as they passed. Whatever the nature of the elk, they had made no mistakes, had offered us no chance to take advantage of them. A false move or slight slip on our part would have sent the jittery elk running in a heartbeat. After yet another wait, we started in slow pursuit, aware that the elk were approaching the safety of a hillside of black timber.

Once there, our chance to see them would be lost. A few hundred yards later, we came to a large circular clearing surrounded by more scattered trees. We knelt behind the protection of a limb-filled pine. We could see no elk, but it felt as though the trees on the far side of the clearing had eyes. We sensed that if we took a single step into that clearing, we would have reached the unsuccessful end of the hunt.

We waited and watched. Then, I decided to gamble on a bugle. Sitting behind Lars, I gave what I hoped would sound like the bugle of the most wimpy, nerdy, and despicable bull who every walked the earth. Immediately, we heard a sound that, at first, we could not identify. The noise was coming from behind the screen of a large tree across the clearing, less than a 150 yards away.

The sound was a combination of loud scraping and of hollow clattering. Then it dawned on us that the noise was that of a bull fighting a tree and rubbing his antlers on the limbs! The bull was mad enough to demolish a tree, but still would not bugle.

I again gave the wimp bugle and again the outraged bull angrily raked the tree. Both the bull and we continued to wait and watch in the silence that followed. With no more trees to cover our movements, we were pinned down, helpless to try to see behind the screen of the tree. It seemed the bull was still not sure if we were a bull or not, but he certainly was not going to make the first move regardless. He was in a safe place, and he knew it.

We heard the bull fight the tree once more while I responded with another wimpy bugle. The clattering of antlers on wood abruptly stopped. The silent moments that followed dragged by slowly as I wondered if the bull had vanished. I thought to myself, "Not now, luck, don't leave us now." Then, suddenly, the bull appeared in an opening as he walked from behind the large tree. Bill and I held our breath as Lars looked at the bull through the scope of his .30-06. At the boom of the rifle and the sound of a bullet slapping meat, the bull stopped. Lars quickly fired a second shot, and the bull dropped to the ground like rock.

It was a breathtaking finish to an extraordinary hunt, a hunt in which we avoided making mistakes due to an equal measure of skill and luck. But then, when you stop to think about it, aren't equal amounts of skill and luck the first things we pack into our duffles before we head for elk camp?

Chapter Four
Expect the Unexpected

Once when I was a lad in my early teens, I received a harsh lesson from a rooster pheasant and a subsequent few words of wisdom from an old hunter. I had been straddling a barbed-wire fence with my shotgun securely leaning against a post. With a remarkable sense of timing, a rooster chose that instant to explode from practically under my nose. I could do nothing but balance on one leg while both hands held down the wire, and I watched the bird sail away until he became a small dot. The old hunter, who watched my embarrassing performance, smiled a knowing smile and said: "Always expect the unexpected."

This advice had proved to be worth all the gold in the world during my years of hunting. Many years and many miles from my teenage pheasant hunting country, it again paid off as Lamar—the moose hunter for whom I was outfitting and guiding—and I approached the bull he had just shot.

Lamar, Meredith, and I had packed our duffle bags, food, canvas wall tent, stove, and other gear on five pack horses and rode twenty miles into the nearby mountains to hunt a moose for Lamar. Although we had known him for several years, we had never hunted with Lamar. He was a skilled and experienced hunter, competent outdoorsman, and delightful camping companion.

Our camp was a snug one. Besides the canvas wall tent, we pitched two small sleeping tents. The canvas wall tent served as the cook tent and included a collaspable tin wood stove, folding table and chairs, and a gas lantern. Meredith's hot, delicious meals were very popular with Lamar and I. The camp was nestled just inside a stand of lodgepole pines and overlooked a large meadow of short willows and grass. A fair-sized, crystal-clear stream furnished both drinking water and constant background music as it splashed over the rocky stream bed. During the hunt, I watched moose and elk from the edge of camp.

On the first day of hunting, Lamar and I walked from camp. Small patches of snow remained in shaded areas, timber, and on north slopes. The breeding season was winding down for the moose, but we hoped to find an amorous bull giving his attentions to the ladies. Walking up the drainage in which we were camped, we slowly hunted along miles of dense timber and willow-filled openings. Two bull elk and a half dozen cow and calf moose were the big-game tally for the day.

The next day's tally was even better as Lamar and I hunted through some of the most majestic scenery and splendid mountains in the world. We started the day by putting away a big breakfast, and then rode several miles from camp. After tying the horses, we worked some timber and small bogs bordering several lakes. It was while creeping through a timber patch that we had some entertainment from a snoozing band of elk.

Elk season was open. I carried an elk tag in my pocket, but because I was guiding, I carried no rifle. Leading the way, I stepped from behind a tree and into full view of a very large bull elk. The bull was dozing in the sun not more than sixty yards away. Lamar quickly followed my action as I knelt behind low bushes and watched the bull—the height of nature's grace, strength, and beauty. The bull's impressive antlers were long tined and especially massive, and every hair of his shiny coat seemed perfectly in place. In a moment, I asked to borrow Lamar's custom-built .270 rifle. Putting the scope's crosshairs on the bedded bull's shoulder, I whispered "bang!," then returned the rifle. Lamar encouraged me to stop pretending and shoot the handsome bull, but I declined. A swirl of wind from us to the cows bedded near the bull alerted the elk and removed the temptation as the band trotted away.

We returned to the horses and rode a short distance to a lake before eating our lunch. As we ate beside the lake, brilliantly colored brook trout slowly patrolled the shore. After lunch, we rode to another area and passed within a stone's throw of several mule deer. The group of does, fawns, and two small bucks didn't seem at all concerned about the hunters and the horses so near to them.

From the top of a cliff overlooking acres of willow bottom and meandering stream, we spotted a half dozen moose. We determined two were bulls, though they were small. Lamar and I both hoped to find something with more antler. We were content to pass the afternoon watching for more moose and enjoying the magnificent surrounding country. That evening at camp, just before dark, I watched two cows and a calf moose browse their way into the meadow among the horses. It was a pleasant sight at the end of a good day of hunting.

The following day, we again rode our saddle horses to a likely area and probed willow-lined stream banks and boggy ponds for a bull moose. There were enough fresh moose tracks to hold our interest constantly. We both were aware that we could run into Mr. Big at any time—which we did, though he was a Mr. Big of the wrong species. As Lamar and I walked along a game trail in timber, I looked up to see another very large bull elk as he came toward us. The bull saw us at the moment we saw him, stopped for a few seconds, and then, with a few quick jumps, was gone. Lamar began to think he had brought the wrong type of tag for our hunt.

By noon, we had reached the heart of a willow-filled meadow surrounded by dense timber. It was perfect habitat for moose, elk, and deer, a fact confirmed by the plentiful fresh tracks pushed into the soft dirt. Finding an ideal place for a picnic, Lamar and I seated ourselves on a sandy strip of land covered with trees. To our backs was the deep stream, to our front was part of the large meadow, and to our right from a thick stand of trees not more than fifty yards away stepped a cow moose!

We had not even taken a bite from our lunches when the cow appeared. As she strode into view, I nudged Lamar and slowly pointed with a sandwich toward her. Lamar calmly traded his lunch for his rifle and waited. Suddenly, a second cow stepped from the trees and, behind her, we saw movement from a third animal. Looking into the shadows with our binoculars, we saw that the third animal was a large bull moose.

The second cow turned and walked back into the timber, and the bull followed. Lamar and I scrambled to find an opening where we could see the moose and get a shot. A narrow lane split the timber, and Lamar quickly sensed that the lane was where the bull would come. He only had time to steady his rifle against a tree before the bull's head and neck appeared in the open lane and stopped.

A fifty-yard shot at a bull moose's neck is not unreasonable and, at the crack of the rifle, the bull dropped like a sack of rocks. I watched through my binoculars for several minutes for any sign of life from the bull, but he never twitched. As I gathered my lunch and gear to walk to the bull, I chuckled to myself: "Can it be this easy?"

The answer was no. I thank my lucky stars that I was expecting the unexpected as we approached the bull. When we were twenty yards from the bull, I jumped from a log laying across a boggy slough and glanced up to see a large bull moose slowly walking away! Did the bull Lamar shot get up? Was there another large bull? Do we dare shoot the standing bull if there is already a dead one lying on the ground?

I quickly turned to Lamar and reported what I had seen. I told him to cover the walking moose with his rifle while I looked for a dead bull. Lamar scrambled for a place to watch the live bull as I raced to the area where he had shot at the bull. To my amazement, there was no dead moose, no blood, nothing at all where the bull had dropped.

"I don't see any bull!," I yelled to Lamar. "The one you're watching must be the one you shot at. Let him have it!"

In the time it took for me to search for a dead bull, the walking bull had traveled nearly a hundred yards through tall willows and scattered trees. The safety of thick, black timber was only a few yards away when Lamar put the bull down for good. As we caped the animal, we found the bullet hole of the first shot. The bullet had missed the vertebra by an inch and had only momentarily paralyzed the moose.

It was the kind of hunting situation that often leads to two dead animals instead of one—or a wounded animal escaping. Our hunt easily could have ended in disaster, except that we had expected the unexpected.

Chapter Five
Pack Trip of Independence

July 4, 1976. Bicentennial parades were organized across our nation, with the Stars and Stripes leading high-stepping baton twirlers, blaring brass bands, tissue-covered floats, and smiling politicians. City parks were crammed with people kneeling over picnic baskets. Cans of cold drinks passed from hand to hand as the country and the world toasted a special "Happy Birthday" to America.

On that day, deep in the Absaroka Mountains, Meredith and I celebrated independence in our own way. Our parade consisted of two riding horses and three pack horses as we picked our way up the rocky bed of a small stream toward a distant mountain pass. We left our timberline camp early with the hope of crossing a large snowfield on the other side of the pass before the snow thawed and softened in the morning sun. Despite our early departure, though, we arrived at a mushy snowfield. As soon as the horses stepped onto the bottomless snow, I knew we were in trouble.

The snowfield was the result of winter winds driving loose snow through the narrow pass and piling it in a deep, sloping drift on the lee side. In it, the horses sank to their cinches, lunging and floundering for solid footing. The last pack horse in the string, a stout sorrel known to buck on occasion, was thrown off balance by his heavy pack and rolled over twice before stopping. Meredith's saddle horse made a series of leaps across the deep drift before pausing. Just as she started to step from the horse, the animal gave another lunge, threw Meredith into its path, and leaped over my still-rolling spouse. When the flying hooves, spraying snow, and profanity subsided, I was relived beyond words to see my bride in one piece, shaken and snow-covered but unharmed. The only casualty was a single broken egg, one of the many dozens we carried in the packs of the big sorrel. I figured the excitement on the slushy snowfield was equal to any fireworks display that day.

We had been out two weeks on a pack trip that would end nearly four months and 500 miles later. With no fixed route or schedule, our plan was to wander around the few remaining fragments of the wilderness in the lower 48 states and experience the sights, sounds, and scenes of wildlands yet unchanged by the hand of man.

What a glorious summer and fall we had in nature's land. Flowers of every brilliant color imaginable filled the meadows, on a carpet of lush, green grass. Silent forests harbored everything from mosquitoes to moose, from field mice to grizzly bears. The high, tundra-like mountaintops were dotted by summering elk. Often we saw the surefooted bighorns moving effortlessly across cliff faces, moose feeding in willow bogs, and graceful mule deer walking silently and listening intently. Clear, cold streams furnished us with drinking water, refreshing swims on hot days, pleasant background music, and tasty meals from their trout-filled pools.

Of course, we had our bad days and our gloomy moments. There were drizzling rains and cold fogs. Man and beast suffered from the biting horseflies and mosquitoes. We were not immune to the bruises, cuts, and scrapes that accompany any pack trip, though we escaped serious mishap. We took the unfortunate and discouraging times in stride; they were nothing compared to the adventures we had.

Our trail rambled through drainages with names that reflected the Western land: the Wind, the Wood, the Greybull, the Shoshone, Deer Creek, Thorofare, Yellowstone, Buffalo Fork, Soda Fork, and Horse Creek. No writer of Western novels could have dreamed up better names for the streams and rivers of that country.

It has been said that necessity is the mother of invention, and we proved it during that trip. We had camped in an open stand of tall lodgepole pines on the banks of the headwaters of the Yellowstone. It was late in the summer, and the biting bugs were nearly gone for the season. Those were lazy days for both the horses and ourselves. A deep pool behind a huge, flat rock was about a hundred yards from camp. In its dark, green depths rested schools of cutthroat trout, while others lazily gulped mayflies from the surface. We were starved for fresh meat, but nothing in the tackle box interested the fussy fish. Spoons and spinners danced by them without effect, and the plump trout were completely indifferent to the small assortment of flies we floated to them. The cutthroats wanted and would accept only mayflies; we had nothing similar. What we did have were some bare hooks, and the determination to put a fresh trout into butter sizzling in the cast-iron skillet.

We crafted our own flies. We cut wings in a small figure-eight pattern from a clear plastic bread bag. Two short fibers of hemp plucked from a lash rope provided the split tails. Brown thread from a small, emergency sewing kit allowed a few wraps, and a moment later we produced our own version of a juicy mayfly. It was dynamite, a complete success for the makeshift, fly-tying rookies. For several days we dined on tasty trout.

During the pack trip, we explored on foot as well as on horseback. At times, we traveled on wheel-used trails, and sometimes we walked where few

Meridith Taylor pauses with horses high in the Wyoming wilderness during a summer pack trip.

people, if any, had ever set foot. Occasionally, we packed to a trailhead and returned to civilization for fresh supplies. They were fun days, care-free days, weeks, months that blended into an incredible, wonderful experience.

Twice we saw the fresh tracks of grizzly bears. One set was embedded in soft dirt near a pile of grizzly droppings so large we jokingly speculated on the possibility of using it as a landmark, and perhaps even going so far as to carve faces on it like at Mt. Rushmore. The other tracks were made in mud and soft snowfields, huge tracks that clearly showed the long, finger-sized claws. These tracks revealed that the bear had approached within a quarter mile of our camp before turning and retracing its steps. I believe the bear had heard our horse bells, wished to avoid humans, and simply left the area. We never saw a grizzly during the trip, but felt a sense of satisfaction from knowing the great bear was near.

One of the few times I have ridden a swimming horse was during that summer. The Forest Service trail we were using crossed a major river drainage. We had ridden down through rimrock and cliffs on a zigzagging, switchback trail and camped near the river. The following morning, we carefully packed the gear to prevent it from getting wet when we crossed the river. The horses entered the water from a gravel bank and waded toward the far side. I watched the water rise to my horse's knees, the cinches, over my boot tops, and nearly to my knees, when suddenly the horse started to float and drift with the current. I could feel the animal's strong paddle as he swam the short distance before again touching bottom. The other horses followed suit and seemed to enjoy the swim.

On several occasions, I noticed that some of our campsites had been used repeatedly for years, and, at a few camps dotted with flakes and chips of flint, chert, and obsidian, for centuries. One campsite had a weathered buffalo skull spiked high in a tree with the inscription: "T. W. 1924," carved into the forehead. Under the skull was another inscription scratched on a thin board from an apple crate: "This skull has been here a long time. Please leave it alone." That request is still being honored today.

Old horseshoes showed that others had used the same camps we used. One evening, we rode to a small grove of aspens near a little spring in a sheltered bowl. The trees were the first we had seen after riding across miles of tundra-like mountaintop. The bowl contained all we required—wood, water, and grass. It was a natural campsite, and as soon as we saw it, we knew it was where we would spend the night. Some of the tree trunks bore scars of various kinds and ages, showing that other people also thought it a good camp. On the ground were hundreds of chips from glass-like igneous rocks, remnants of the bow-and-arrow and buffalo days. In a short time, I found a small scraper made from petrified wood, proving the old-timers also had considered the camp a good spot. I spent many hours looking for evidence of fire-rings, tent poles, and litter, and speculated on the era and character of yesteryear's campers.

We explored one of the major drainages with special interest. It had been hunted and written about in 1930 by a man named Grancel Fitz. Fitz was an avid trophy hunter, one of the creators of the original Boone and Crocket scoring system for big-game animals. I had read the accounts of his fascinating elk hunt in the drainage and compared his reports to the country I saw nearly fifty years later. Mr. Fitz said he had hunted on nine days and had seen eighty-four bull elk, of which thirty-four were six-pointers or bigger. There were, according to Fitz, many times that number of cow elk, fifty-six mule deer, sixteen moose, and no other hunters. To top that off, he shot a huge bull elk with seventeen total points and a sixty-five-inch spread. His story made me yearn for the good old days. The country looked the same, for the most part, but the hunting had changed dramatically. The creeks that Fitz had hunted now were heavily hunted each fall, and six-point elk were scarce. If Mr. Fitz saw the country today and thought about the spectacular adventure he had in 1930, I imagine he would sell his hunting rifle and take up another sport.

Though the hunting had changed, the country had not; it still had a wealth of wildlife and wildlands. Meredith and I spent a wonderful summer seeing the same sights that the first settlers, mountain men, and Indians saw.

Chapter Six
Doing It Right

I have evolved into a fussy, seemingly hard-to-please hunter. I strive to make my hunts special so that I can recall them as cherished memories. I have a check list of standards, almost a formula, with which to measure the quality of my hunts: Did I capture an adventure? Did I go afield with the reverence animals deserve? Did I conduct myself as a sportsman or was I a slob with a gun? Did I set a good example for others, especially the young and the non-hunters?

If I can satisfy this code, it doesn't matter whether I ever fire a shot or kill my quarry. It doesn't matter if I hunt from a vehicle or twenty-five miles from a road. Nor it does it matter if I hunt alone or with a crowd.

Through the years, I have shot big antelope, small antelope, old and young, bucks and does. I have killed running antelope, standing antelope, close antelope, and distant antelope. Then one day, it dawned on me that, with few exceptions, I could recall few details of my past antelope hunts. All I remembered was that I went hunting, shot an antelope, and came home. I was doing it all wrong. I was not an antelope hunter; I was merely an antelope killer.

To remedy this, I intently studied maps and filled out antelope applications a few days later. I got lucky with the drawing and received a license; the stage was set. I started preparing for an antelope adventure, and was determined to do it right.

It was two weeks into the hunting season before I loaded the last box of gear into the camper shell of my pickup and wheeled my outfit down the highway. I had chosen my hunting area with care. Many of the state's antelope herds had been reduced during a severe winter two years before and were still recovering. The area I had picked had been spared during that killing winter and offered as good of a chance as any for older bucks. During the summer months, I had scouted the hunting area twice. To my delight, I had seen many mature black-horned bucks among the herds.

Another important factor in my choice was that the area was dominated by publicly owned land administered by the Bureau of Land Management. I do not mind asking for permission to hunt private lands, but I cherish the freedom of hunting on public land—my land.

I made up my mind that I would hunt until I found an exceptional, large-horned, old buck. By setting this standard, I would make the hunt more of a challenge—a special memory. A mental picture of the buck I would accept was programmed into my brain, a measure that proved invaluable as I glassed and evaluated bucks throughout the hunt. Data on horn length, prong length, base circumference, and symmetry were fed into the computer between my ears. If this "biocompute" gave a negative read-out, I would just walk away and look for another buck.

Three hours of highways were behind me when I turned into a small town bordering my hunting area. I chatted with the grocery clerk, a gas-station attendant, a couple of ranch hands, and other local folks, hoping to gain information about camping sites, reports of elusive monster pronghorns, and tips about traditional hunting spots.

The response I received was bored and indifferent. After a little refection, I understood why. The town's residents literally saw antelope from their doorsteps 365 days a year. Their dogs barked at the animals during the summer. In the winter, antelope were herded from the streets and back into the sagebrush. During hard times, antelope were these people's mainstay, and I surmised the only reason why most of these locals even worked at all was because they loathed a steady diet of antelope meat. I remained undaunted, though. I had driven less than a half mile from town when I spotted antelope. Four hundred yards on one side of the road was a single doe; eighty yards on the other side was a mature buck with seven does. Through my binoculars, I examined the buck.

The proximity of the small town triggered my common sense, and my fussy conscience reasoned that if I shot a twelve-inch, so-so buck three minutes into the hunt, then my trip would fall far short of the mark I had set for myself. My biocomputer flashed negative, and I headed for other hunting grounds. I spent several hours rambling around endless miles of deeply carved, rolling sagebrush plains. Occasional pine and cedar-covered rocky outcroppings rose high above the terrain, excellent places for spotting-scope sessions. By mid-afternoon, I had watched several golden eagles, an emaciated, mangy coyote, three distant vehicles that appeared to be carrying hunters, a suitable campsite in prime antelope country, and countless antelope of both sexes and all ages. I had seen perhaps thirty bucks, many of them mature herd bucks with horns more than a foot long. Each one I rejected; none met my expectations.

Back at the parked vehicle, I wolfed down a sandwich while I continued to glass the area. I kept binoculars and spotting scope at hand constantly to watch the movements of antelope here, identify a new animal there, and scan everywhere.

With only two hours of daylight remaining, I began walking toward an area that looked promising. The terrain was cut with many deep, steep-sided gullies and isolated from the roads by the sweeping arch of a sandstone bluff and an alkali seep that stretched for miles. It seemed to be a likely place for an educated buck. A cold, stiff wind began to blow, drawing down an overcast sky. What a contrast hunting antelope in that area was to other hunts I had experienced. With nearly all other big game, I have spent days trying to locate even a glimpse of the animals I sought. During this hunt, though, I was almost constantly in sight of at least one antelope, if not dozens. The rut had not ended, so the bucks were moving constantly. It proved wise for me to stay alert and watch the crests of draws and the skyline. Many times bucks strolled into view and past me on their search for does. I tracked more than one unsuspecting, romantic-minded buck with the crosshairs of my rifle scope as he promenaded past. Near the center of an isolated landscape below the sandstone bluff was a large ridge covered with waving grass. Lying down with only her back and head exposed was a doe, completely spent from running. Thirty feet from her, a heavy-horned buck panted. His sides were heaving and his head was lowered between his front legs.

If the buck's horns had not been so intriguing, I might have taken more time to observe the courting rituals of pronghorns, but my main interest was to get the buck in the field of my spotting scope. Across a considerable distance, the horns did not appear very long, but they were thick, with well-developed prongs. My biocomputer signaled: "Maybe. More data needed. Get closer." As I began studying the sagebrush country for a stalk, the doe suddenly jumped to her feet and fled. The buck tried to herd the doe to the east but she insisted on going west. With the buck like a mirror-image of the doe, the pair ran, leaped, spun, and raced in perfect unison. Around and around, back and forth they flew in a breathtaking, beautiful, high-speed ballet. Finally, the pronghorns vanished miles away in a maze of gullies, occasional puffs of dust marking their trail. I never saw that buck again.

Now it was time to head to camp. A race ensued to see if darkness, a snow squall, or I would reach the camper first. The snow squall won, hands down. I faced squarely into the driving flakes, but still managed to see several bunches of antelope before they saw me. Cussing the snow-dotted lenses of my binoculars, I appraised the bucks in each bunch. I was a half mile from the shelter of my pickup when a string of antelope filed from a large draw six hundred yards away. The fading light, combined with the white-out of the storm, made the light-colored antelope look like eerie shadows, sagebrush phantoms. Thirty animals materialized; five were large, older bucks. Four of them carried horns in the twelve- to thirteen-inch range—run-of-the-mill bucks like those I had been passing up all day. The fifth was noticeably larger.

I was concealed where I knelt, but couldn't move in any direction without being seen by the herd. Finally, the animals moved beyond the crest of the draw. I started off at a trot, covered the six hundred yards, and peeked over the crest. Across a flat covered with low sagebrush, the herd milled—about six hundred yards away. In the dim light and distance, I still was not sure the biggest buck was the one I wanted. I detected a slight depression in the flat winding its way toward the herd. I cradled my rifle and started belly-crawling through the snow-covered dust. The herd had fanned out by the time I crawled to within a hundred and fifty yards. With marginal light, frozen knees and hands, and wary eyes an all sides of me, I was in trouble. Then the biggest buck, a silhouette, trotted into view. His horns were long and massive. In a slumped, half-kneeling position, I tried to steady the floating crosshairs. Holding the rifle to my shoulder, I quietly whispered, "Bang." I just was not comfortable or confident with the shot, and turned it down.

I snaked my way back down the depression and jogged to the pickup. There was no question as to where I would be at daylight. I was determined to find that buck again. The delightful Indian summer of the previous days had lulled me into packing light clothes as well as my summer-weight bedroll. Oh, how I paid for my carelessness as I lay shivering in the camper shell that night! I'm fairly certain I would have slept warmer in a deep freeze. What an added sweetness the glow of the eastern horizon has after such a night.

Breakfast was more for ceremony than nutrition. I gnawed on a couple of frozen donuts and chased them down with coffee. Long before adequate shooting light, I shouldered my rifle and started walking. Before I had gone fifty yards, the wheezing cough of an alarmed antelope sounded from a short distance away. "This isn't proper," I told myself. "I can't even get out of camp before I'm up to my ears in antelope." Common sense and prudence told me I was twenty minutes too early and too eager. I slipped back to the pickup and gnawed on a couple more donuts.

When it was fully light, I placed my spotting scope on the hood of the pickup and surveyed the world in all directions. Under a clear blue sky, there were antelope everywhere. The closest, a doe a hundred yards away, alternated between staring at me and watching five does trailed by a small buck casually walking a little way in front of my vehicle. I checked the area where I had seen the big buck at dark. There, looking like little specks, I saw thirty animals, five with the telltale black heads of large bucks. I quickly left camp and soon was swallowed by the rolling, broken prairie.

If there ever was a case of too many animals, that was the day. From the time I started walking until the early afternoon when I peeked over a grassy rise and saw the tremendous pronged horns of a buck towering above the sagebrush where he was bedded, I was in danger of spooking antelope. I skirted many bunches and looked over a number of nice bucks as I made my way toward the herd of thirty with the five large bucks.

Approaching within a thousand yards of them, I carefully checked the herd with the spotting scope. I failed to get a clear, detailed look at the largest buck's horns until then. He was a dandy—thick, symmetrical horns showed off the large, well-formed prongs. He was unquestionably the best buck I had seen. The data of the buck's heavy bases, massive prongs, and well-curved horns was fed into my biocomputer. The readout clicked: "Yes, definitely." My common sense reminded me that this was the largest buck of the more than fifty I had seen during the last two days and urged me to go for it. My standards of a special hunt were already satisfied.

I had no sooner made the decision to try for the large buck and put my spotting scope away when, a hundred and twenty five yards to my side, another very large, very impressive buck strode boldly over the skyline and stopped beneath the horizon to stare head-on at me. The black-faced buck seemed more curious than alarmed; his shiny, long horns were awesome and almost made my eyes pop out. I slowly and deliberately rested my rifle on the metal frame of my pack, chambered a cartridge, and set the crosshairs on the lower throat of the easily 16- or 17-inch buck. Then, as he turned sideways and started walking slowly, my hopes collapsed. Long though his horns were, they also were pathetically thin. The buck's prongs were disappointingly small and poorly developed. I covered the buck's heart with my crosshairs for practice until he was out of sight, then studied the thousand yards of sagebrush between me and the herd with the heavy-horned buck.

By the time I finished covering those thousand yards, I had added a few more antelope to the total headcount. When I peeked from my ambush position, not an antelope was to be seen; the herd had vanished. I quickly, carefully climbed to the top of a nearby hill and glassed for the missing herd. A mile and a half away, I focused on the unmistakable, heavy-horned buck driving six does toward the base of a pine-covered ridge. For some unknown reason, the seven had split from the herd, a circumstance in my favor. The large buck seemed to be forcing the six does into a small, sagebrush-filled draw cutting into the rough ridge. I sat biding my time, watched the big buck's efforts, and scanned in a 360-degree circle for more antelope. Finally, the buck and does disappeared behind a curve of the distant draw and I started in pursuit.

It was well past noon when I approached the place where I had last seen the big buck. At that point, I avoided what could have been a costly mistake. From the cover of the pine-dotted ridge, I spied a bunch of antelope—six does and a large buck moving across a grassy slope five hundred yards below me. An island of huge boulders and weather-tortured limber pines was between the animals and me. The antelope walked and trotted toward the island from one side while I ran in a crouched position toward the island from the opposite side. The swift prairie racers beat me to the rocky knoll, but I held the advantage by seeing them first. I had just reached the first of the barrel-sized rocks when I noticed the back of a grazing doe not forty-five yards away. Caught in the open, I quickly sat down and raised my rifle. A split second later, the doe raised her head and walked into full view. Other does with large, fluid eyes and delicate legs followed, grazing directly toward me. At last, a set of handsome black horns floated above a large, table-like boulder.

I sat on bare earth, fully exposed, with five hundred square inches of blaze orange and both hands full of shiny wood and blue steel. Twenty-five yards away grazed a group of high-strung, keen-eyed, nervous pronghorns, looking directly at me, then looking away as if I were one of the lifeless rocks. It was a tense moment. I would have eagerly traded my rifle for my bow just then. The buck stood sideways and stared at my motionless form for what seemed like minutes. I dared not even blink as I looked from his horns to his eyes. My biocomputer flashed an urgent message—something was wrong. The buck carried 13- to 14- inch horns, with good prongs and average thickness. He was a splendid buck, though not exceptional. Some uneasy feeling made me realize the buck standing twenty-five yards in front of my rifle's muzzle was not the one I had come to hunt, not the animal I had come to kill. I remained still and mulled over the possibilities of what had happened. Either I had misjudged the buck as I watched him earlier through the spotting scope or there were two separate bunches of antelope in the area, both composed of six does and one large buck. The latter thought seemed incredible, but the more I studied the nearby buck, the more I became convinced he was not the same antelope I had seen earlier.

The bunch grazed past me, the buck still unaware how close he had been to death. When the antelope had moved off about a hundred yards, I stood up to watch their reaction. Instantly, they were on the run and soon disappeared over a distant horizon. I stood watching the buck fade into the skyline while wondering if I had done the right thing. Determined to see if there was another group of seven antelope nearby, I again set out.

I tried to move like the shadow of a hunting bobcat along the base of the ridge and into a sagebrush draw. Ahead, just over the crest of a brushy rise, rocked the coal-black horns of a buck—*the* buck—as he lay chewing his cud. At ninety yards, the heavy horns were more impressive than ever. Things were going my way, and I didn't want to turn the tables. I simply sat on a flat rock, held the rifle across my knees, and waited. For what seemed like hours, I watched the beautiful horns gently shake back and forth.

Suddenly, without warning, the buck stood up, took two quick steps down the slope, and disappeared. I nearly screamed in frustration. Then, just as suddenly, the buck reappeared, walking broadside along the crest of the rise. My crosshairs had only enough time to find his shoulder before he stopped behind a tall sagebrush with only his white rump exposed. I was getting exasperated. A second later, he stepped two paces into full view and lay down, facing directly at me. I don't know if he ever saw me or not, for I never gave him time to react. As his weight settled onto the ground, my rifle spoke. The buck rolled on his side, slowly kicked twice, and died. Six does burst past the buck, running down the draw.

I admired the handsome buck, signed my hunting license, snapped a few token photos, and field dressed the animal. On a whim, I stood above the animal and glassed with my binoculars a 180-degree arc. A total of seventy-three antelope were grazing, resting, or walking within my field of vision. I started for the pickup with special memories and the satisfaction of having done it right.

Chapter Seven
Give Him A Day

 What shall I give one small boy?
A glamorous game, a tinseled toy?
A barlow knife, a puzzle pack?
A train that runs on curving track?
A picture book, a real live pet....
No, there's plenty of time for such things yet.
Give him a day for his very own—
just one small boy and his Dad alone.
A walk in the woods, a romp in the park,
a fishing trip from dawn to dark.
Give the gift that only you can—
the companionship of his Old Man.
Games are outgrown, and toys decay,
but he'll never forget if you "give him a day."

Author Unknown

The worth of memories, the personal value of any hunting, fishing, or camping trip can only be calculated after it is over. Only after the guns, rods, and smoke-blackened cooking utensils have been put away can you sit back and sort out the positive and negative aspects of the experience. The time to reflect on and remember those golden highlights is upon your return home.

In the spring of 1992, five others and I experienced an adventure of great value during a fishing trip to northern Saskatchewan, a trip that will hold greater value to me than the sum of its individual parts.

The trip started in Wyoming when my friend, Tim, mentioned that he, his 12-year-old son Andy, our mutual friend, John, and John's teen-age son, Johnnie, were driving to northern Canada to fish. Tim wondered if I wanted to go along. Silly question. With one seat still available, I asked if my Dad could be the sixth person on our adventure.

It didn't take much to persuade Dad to join. I left a message on his answering machine outlining the details. When Dad returned my call a few hours later, his first words were, "When are we leaving?" A few weeks later, three father-son pairs loaded their gear into a crowded vehicle and headed to parts unknown.

It was a long journey north. Late May often is a time that is something between winter and spring. We drove through the high plains where the landscape was dominated by neither the patches of white snow nor the brilliant green of new grass. It was hard to determine whether the farmers still locked out of their fields by mud and ice or the migrating birds looking for nesting places were the most impatient for warm weather. Mile after mile of rolling prairie, timber-filled river bottoms, immaculate farms dotting rich dark soil, and the occasional town flashed past the windows. The international border crossing was as fast and routine as our stops for gas at convenience stores.

Only after we left the last paved road and strings of power poles behind did the country take on a sense of wildness. Two components were present: a monoculture of short, moss-covered pine trees and an incredible amount of water. No other features could be found, but in the many murky rivers and lakes we passed, we sensed an unseen treasure of savage fighting fish just waiting for our lures. Our excitement peaked as the long trip finally drew to a close.

Our adventure really began the morning we carried our gear down the loading dock of a remote, well-planned fishing and hunting lodge. At the end of the dock waited a vintage, but reliable Beaver float plane. Across the bay from the dock was half a mile of dark, newly opened water, a contrast to the white, frozen lake just beyond. The cold of winter had only released its frozen grip on the lakes during the last few days.

The lodge itself was a classic, with its log structures, moose antlers on the outside ridge poles, inside decor of mounted fish and animals, and every item needed to separate comfort from mere survival, life from death in that isolated region. As could be expected from a first-class operation, the lodge was family owned and family run. We enjoyed a relaxed, pleasant breakfast among ourselves, other anglers and the owners before making a last check of our gear. I explained to one of the owners that I was used to catching one- to two-pound trout at home. When he explained that he would be disappointed if I didn't catch and release at least twenty or thirty fish that would swallow a two-pound fish whole, I realized that I was getting into a different class of fishing than I had ever experienced.

The Beaver shuttled our fishing expedition to another lake known for its northern pike. The lodge owners had built a small dock and rustic cabin and had flown in two aluminum motor boats. The six of us were dropped at the dock—miles across bog, marsh, muskeg, and countless lakes from the nearest sign of civilization. Things were beginning to look up.

It didn't take long for us to toss our gear into the cabin and head for the boats. A few hundred yards from the cabin was a small bay. Into one corner of the bay flowed a creek, tiny enough to step across. Dwarf birch trees hung protectively over the stream. This tiny bay was our first stop in search for fish. Our lures had barely hit the tea-colored water at the mouth of the creek before they were slammed by pike. Huge pike. Pike with incredible rows of needle-like teeth, disagreeable dispositions, and strength.

There is a look in the eyes of a pike that haunts me. It's the same stare that a rattlesnake has when it's disturbed. The message sent from the angry eyes of subdued pike as they glare up from the water comes across in no uncertain terms: "Give me a chance and I'll get even."

The lake we fished was managed under a catch-and-release plan. The plan was a good one, but following the plan was sometimes a challenge. Trying to release the powerful fish was like trying to snatch a diamond ring from a running kitchen garbage disposal. Despite gloves, needle-nosed pliers, and other protection, we all came home with slow healing battle wounds. The phrase "The fish were really biting" took on a whole new meaning.

With each new fish that doubled a rod, our group of pike fighters drifted further away from the thoughts and worries of the world of deadlines and telephones. We tried numerous parts of the ten-mile-long lake and discovered all of them contained red-hot fishing. Three fathers and three sons became the only people in a universe no bigger than a lake, a cabin, and two small boats. Often when on hunting or fishing trips, one special event, a solo sentence, or a single moment will galvanize the entire experience and condense the combined pleasure of the trip into a long-remembered golden moment. Such a moment happened for me on the third day of this fishing trip.

The sky had changed from a promising, spring blue to a threatening, cold-front gray. Our addiction to the adrenaline rush caused by the jerk of the rods and the thrashing fish had not yet been satisfied, and the change in the weather did not diminish the aggressiveness of the pike. Dad and I had gone fishing alone. From a boat, we fished our way up a deep channel to another small lake. Yard-long pike were numerous, and as quickly as we could release one, another was on the line.

We slowly trolled, not because it was any more productive than any other method, but because it was the way Dad had always fished and still preferred. I was content to pilot the boat and let my father concentrate on fishing just as he had piloted for me during fishing trips so many years before. The putt, putt, putt of the small gas motor was the only sound in a windless world as our boat pushed a circle in the lake's calm water.

There were no long pauses or rests between fish. Instead, it seemed that no sooner would we release a fish, start moving again, and get our lines in the water, than another fish would strike. More times than imaginable, both of our rods bent and shook from the tugging of heavy fish at the same time. Then, suddenly, time seemed to stop. It was as if God had suddenly halted the world, reached down with his hand to grab a small piece of creation containing only a father and son in a little boat on a small lake, and examined it. His examination revealed a happy pair, grateful for the company of each other and filled with the peace that can only be found in silent places. I caught myself happily daydreaming about nothing in particular, but grateful for a moment alone with my father. In a moment, I acknowledged that golden moment with a slight smile and light heart, snapped out of what seemed like a trance, and again heard the putt, putt, putt of the motor.

Only too soon did the time arrive when the Beaver airplane glided to the dock in front of the lake's cabin and carried us back to civilization. The long drive home was mixed with laughter as stories of the last few days were retold and relived, silent meditation as we raced away from one world back to a much different one, and periods of trying to put into words the feelings we had shared as fathers, sons, and friends. Somewhere along the way, I showed Dad the poem, "Give Him a Day" from a travel handout I picked up along the way. He read the lines and replied: "It goes both ways."

Chapter Eight
Friendship Elk Hunt

 We were having one of those rare, dry autumns. It was past the second week of November, but there was virtually no new snow in the high mountains. I blew the steam from my second cup of coffee and studied the calendar on the cabin wall. I was startled when I realized there were only a few days of elk season remaining, and I had yet to put an elk in the freezer for winter's meat. The situation called for action; I hopped into my pickup and drove the mile or so to my friend's cabin.

"Dave," I said, "do you realize there are only a few days of elk season left?"

"Yep."

"Do you have an elk yet?"

"Nope."

"You want to go hunting back in the hills tomorrow?"

"Yep."

"Do you mind if I invite Tim along?"

"Nope."

"Good. I've only got three pack horses plus my saddle horse. You two will have to bring your own saddle horses. We'll have to travel light in case we get more than one elk."

"Okay."

Dave frequently conversed in one-word sentences. It had something to do with the solitude of the long Wyoming winters.

We decided to meet at my place early the next morning. Both Dave and I had guided elk hunters that fall for different outfitters, but had not yet had the opportunity to hunt for ourselves. We were not allergic to beef, but it went against our grain to not try to fill the larder with wild meat. Also, guides' wages dictated hamburger and spare ribs; we were partial to thick round steaks, backstrap roasts, and tenderloin.

Tim was a new acquaintance of mine. I did not know much about him, but the few times I had visited with him made me think I would enjoy hunting with him. He recently immigrated to the United States from India, and the two of us had coincidentally moved to the same small town in Wyoming. I knew he was an avid hunter and sensed he would enjoy the experience of using horses to hunt elk in the mountains of America. When I phoned to invite him, I could tell he was delighted.

Over the phone, we organized the hunt. I knew he had an unfilled elk license. He figured he could borrow a horse, saddle, and scabbard and be at my place at daylight with his gear. He mentioned that he didn't own a sleeping bag, so I told him I would toss in an extra one for him.

The following morning, the three of us had a pleasant trip into the mountains. You couldn't trust the blue sky and semi-bare mountains that late in the fall, and we expected a blizzard to come roaring across the horizon at any time.

Somewhere along the way, I suddenly realized I had forgotten to bring the extra bedroll for Tim. With pack tarps and saddle pads, we decided we could do without it. It would have taken more than the lack of a mere sleeping bag to cause any concern among our jolly group. We were kings of all we surveyed, and rode with the same spirit and sense of freedom as the mountain men of the 1800s. We moved through a treeless pass and descended into the valley below. After traveling nearly eighteen miles, we chose a campsite near the area we planned to hunt.

The site wasn't perfect. The main distraction was a leaning, dead tree directly over the center of our camp, but we reasoned that since it had been there for many years, it would probably stay in place for a few more days. Dave and I each took charge of the principal camp chores. His responsibility was the care of the horses, which wasn't too difficult there because of the ample grass and water a few paces from camp.

My duty as camp cook was reduced to an easy task by the fact that we had brought very little food and cooking gear. Tim was elected to help wherever he thought appropriate. He spent a lot of time asking questions, watching, and learning. I offered to draw straws with Tim to see who would use the bed roll I had brought for myself. He lost, so we gave him most of the saddle pads and canvas pack covers. He soon had a cozy bed near the fire.

It didn't really matter what kind of bed roll any of us had that night, for two reasons. The first was the game we began to play shortly after dark. A strong wind started to blow, and the leaning tree over our heads began to rock. Had we been in real danger, we would have moved but, instead, we made a game out of the swaying snag. The game was a form of "chicken' or "Russian Roulette." Each time the tree creaked and groaned, we laughed, but I'm certain that if there had been a sudden pop and snap of wood, three blurs would have abandoned camp at top speed.

The second reason we didn't sleep much that night was the most memo-

The horses grazed a stones throw from camp.

rable part of the hunt: The three of us preferred to stay awake and talk around the fire. Rarely in my life had I ever enjoyed such comradeship, shared so many common interests, and felt such satisfaction from a conversation. One-word sentences were not in style that night. Our talk naturally revolved around hunting. Dave and I related our adventures in the Rocky Mountains, while Tim fascinated us with stories about hunting in India. From our campfire, we tested rifles, broke horses, killed cobras, measured elk racks, were charged by tigers, caught fish, tracked wounded gaur, trapped coyotes, saw the burning green eyes of leopards, stalked antelope on two continents, watched grizzlies, rode elephants, photographed bighorn sheep, found jungle watering holes, and cautiously rode by angry cow moose. We circled the globe and shared a remarkable night.

A few hours before dawn, it was time to focus our attention on the present hunt. I fixed a breakfast whose only virtue was that it was hot. Tim helped Dave catch and saddle our three riding horses. In a cheerful mood, we rode from camp in the dark twilight of morning. The sky was clear but the wind was fast and bitter cold. We had barely reached timberline when Dave spotted elk.

"Hold up," he said, and stepped from his horse to glass a hillside a half mile away. "There are elk over there."

"Great!," I said.

"A whole herd," he added.

"Good."

"They haven't seen us."

"Terrific."

"Some are lying down."

"Wonderful."

"Be better to leave the horses here."

"Fantastic."

Tim didn't know what to make our of jovial mood, but followed suit as Dave and I tied our horses to trees. The stalk that followed was merry. The Marx Brothers, W. C. Fields, and Charlie Chaplin would have been envious of our performance. We giggled, did Vietnam belly-crawls with knives between our teeth for effect, and flipped coins at junctures to decide the best route. Often, the three of us simultaneously snuck along three independent routes.

Our light-hearted stalk was not without merit, however, and shortly the three of us slowly moved into shooting position less than a hundred yards from the unsuspecting herd. Our comical mood then changed into serious concentration and deadly intent.

Even though the swirling wind threatened to alarm the herd, we laid behind low limbs and watched the elk for a short while. Finally, a spike became uneasy and stood. Dave's rifle boomed, and the spike loped in a tight circle before he collapsed. The herd instantly ran into a compact milling bunch. Tim and I dared not shoot until the elk moved apart. I noticed a fair set of white-tipped antlers in the middle of the bunch as I waited for an elk, any elk, to step into the clear. The lead cow finally led the herd up the slope and the elk strung into a line. The angel of the hunt smiled upon us all and two dry cows fell a short distance from the dead spike. No canned meat and bacon this winter; it would be T-bones and sirloins for us.

We were less than an hour's walk from our camp. I volunteered to pack one of the elk to camp on two of the saddle horses, then return with my pack horses. I had optimistically carried an axe and sling rope in case one of us killed an elk. My horse was a dependable rope horse, and I used him to skid the three elk to a level spot behind a group of trees that protected us from the icy wind. Tim, standing with his hands in the pockets of his down parka, announced his contribution to the elk packing would be to build a warming fire. A lifetime accumulation of deep scars and many poorly healed broken fingers in Tim's hands resulted in restricted circulation and reduced his fingers to painful, nearly useless appendages when exposed to the cold. A warming fire away from the cutting, icy wind certainly seemed in order.

We soon had one of the elk quartered and slung on riding saddles. I left the others to gut and quarter the remaining two elk while I returned to camp.

As I approached camp, I walked past one of my picketed pack horses—
a young, snorty bay gelding. When the horse spotted the elk quarters on the
horses, he suddenly decided the end of the world was near. He snorted loudly
and ran wild-eyed at the end of his rope. After I unloaded the meat, I walked
over to have a chat with the horse and smeared a handful of blood on his nose.
"You may as well get used to it," I told him, "cause we've got more work to do
today."

The gelding got used to packing elk, and by the end of the afternoon, we
had three elk at our leaning-tree camp.

We had six loads of meat and six strong horses. I contemplated packing
our saddle horses, distributing our meager camp among the lighter loads, then
walking out. There was one main problem with the plan; his name was Dave.

Dave was a cowboy. Cowboys do not walk. The entire time we packed the
elk to camp, I wondered if I could persuade Dave to give up his horse without
insulting his wild, wooly, Western image. It was a challenge I couldn't refuse.

My chance presented itself when we returned to camp with the remaining
elk. Much to our surprise, Meredith was there. She had walked the eighteen
miles to our camp because she had seen the bedroll I had forgotten to pack for
Tim and decided to bring it to us. I think the main reason she had come was
just for the heck of it; neither of us needed much of an excuse to go to the hills.
I now had the leverage I needed to try to unhorse a horseman.

I reasoned to Dave that if a frail female could walk to camp, then a healthy
young man like him could walk out. Dave couldn't argue with this male-
chauvinistic logic, but refused to take responsibility if his snaky horse refused
to carry elk and bucked off the load.

Dave's horse, like the others, did its job well, and the following day six
horse loads of winter's meat started the trip to the freezer.

Chapter Nine
Brother Bob Hunts Sheep

Only a few weeks remained of a busy and eventful summer. Meredith and I had bought some land and worked like slaves to build a cabin on it before winter. We spent most of the long, hot summer days fencing, pouring concrete, gathering house logs, and constructing the cabin. In the middle of it all, my brother, Bob, arrived for a visit and announced he had drawn a bighorn sheep license. He wondered if I wanted to go along; I asked when we were going to leave.

I was fairly familiar with the area for which my brother had drawn his permit. For several years, I had hunted in the area and had taken a interest in bighorn sheep. I had applied for and drawn a bighorn license myself several years earlier. During my hunt, I had received an education about bighorn, most of it from the sheep themselves. I made several blunders, walked when I should have glassed, and let eagerness overwhelm good judgment. The rams showed me my errors by disappearing from the area, leaving me to study my foolishness. Failure is a wonderful teacher, and I learned my lessons well. I missed chances at splendid rams, but finally connected with a medium-sized one. Most important, I was a wiser sheep hunter and badly bitten by the sheep-hunting bug.

We immediately started to organize our trip and put together our outfit. Bob's girlfriend, Frances, volunteered to go along as camp cook and offered the use of her horse. Frances's bay gelding was known to possess a few peculiar characteristics. It was rumored the horse once bucked off the same man seventeen times in seventeen miles. The gelding had endured a hard life and remained as unpredictable as a colt.

Bob owned two horses. One was a huge, long-legged sorrel gelding. If the sorrel's brain had been in proportion to the rest of his body, the horse would have been able to read and write. Unfortunately he seemed to suffer from the brontosaurus syndrome—his brain shrank as his body grew. I never fully trusted the sorrel, and every time I climbed on him, I wondered if he would remember that he was supposed to be gentle. As it turned out, the mountain of horse never erupted with me on him.

59

Bob's other horse was much different. He was a small, gray gelding named Smokey—intelligent and tough as a bucket of nails. I originally owned Smokey and rode him from central Colorado to northwestern Wyoming. After five hundred miles, he was as game as ever and ready to travel another five hundred miles. Great horses are a pleasure to own, and smokey was among the best.

One of the true pleasures of the hunt took place in a general store a few days before we left for the mountains. We had gone to town to buy supplies and to visit with the owners, Frank and Alta. The store was unique, a classic general store that blended the pioneer era with the space age. A person could find the latest flashy fashions and sugar-coated kids' breakfast cereals of questionable nutrition, as well as new horse collars and cast-iron Dutch ovens. Our shopping list was long and varied: food from soup to nuts, horseshoes and nails, fishing lures, sling rope, cape salt, horse grain, stove pipe, plastic utensils, and candles. By the time we finished piling supplies on the counter, we lacked only the medicinal spirits which weren't sold in that store.

Frank was a hard-core sheep hunter and had searched the mountains for rams when the term "Grand Slam" still referred to baseball. He had several fine ram heads on his store's walls. His sheep-hunting days were over, but he still loved to talk about them. There was nothing I enjoyed more than to fan the flames of Frank's sheep-hunting memories and watch him get a dreamy, far-away look in his eyes.

"Frank, why don't you come along and show us where to get a ram like that one?," I asked, pointing to a breathtaking bighorn on the wall above us. He laughed and used one of the strategically placed cardboard wastebaskets as a spittoon.

"No, boys, I'm too old for that. Besides, they don't make 'em like that ram anymore." Frank stared out the window at dreams of his youth while Bob and I studied the ram on the wall.

Suddenly, Frank's wife and past sheep-hunting partner, Alta, came buzzing up to us. Opposites attract, and where Frank was easy-going and deliberate, Alta was constantly rushing around the store. She paused to visit with us and ask about Bob's sheep hunt. I knew she had a weakness for sheep hunting too, and just to watch her reaction, I asked, "Why don't you and Frank come along?"

She didn't answer immediately but stared at the counter top in a melancholy trance. Slowly and softly, she said, "I'd love to, I'd really love to."

Just then, another customer rang the hurry-up bell at the meat counter and Alta snapped back to life like a racehorse released from the starting gate. She zoomed off, calling over her shoulder, "but we can't afford to close the store and can't get anyone to run it and...."

Two days before the season opened, we arose at 4:30 a.m. and left for the mountains. Leading the three pack horses on foot, we were eager to begin. The route we took was not the usual trail we followed to the hunting area. We decided to try what appeared to be a shorter, more direct approach—straight up the side of a mountain and then down the other side. The proposed path rose over five thousand feet in elevation and proved to be an exhausting trip that took two days of travel—twice as long as we had planned. It was not without merit, however, and we enjoyed exploring new territory. The most interesting part of the journey was studying the different types of terrain as we climbed. We started beside a fair-sized river that carved its way through eroded sandstone and multicolored badlands. Cottonwood trees and irrigated hay meadows bordered the river. We soon climbed to rolling hills of sagebrush, sparce grass, and juniper trees. We traveled through scattered limber pines before entering the thick, dense forest of pine, spruce, and fir.

Occasionally, we moved into a grassy meadow amid the timber. In the afternoon, we paused beside a stream at timberline. The cool air was fragrant with willows, flowers, and lush grass—a sharp contrast to the hot, dusty air of the sagebrush country below. We climbed to a high pass and crossed through a world of harsh climate, short grass, and tiny, delicate flowers. I marveled at the small blossoms that sprang up at the edge of the receding snow drifted by last winter's storms. It was nearly September, yet it was only springtime for those late arrivals.

We didn't descend the pass but instead traveled at about the same elevation along the rolling mountains for several miles. We were forced to zig-zag across the slope to avoid numerous rocky outcroppings that were danger-ous for horses. Soon it was late afternoon, and it was clear we would not be able to make as many miles as we had planned. We worked our way down the mountain until we reached timberline and found a suitable overnight camp. The sky turned a beautiful pink as we unpacked the horses. We had been traveling for more than ten hours through steep, mostly uphill country. It was a tough day for man and beast. Frances quickly dug through one of the packs like a badger digging for ground squirrels and came up with the snake-bite bottle. She announced a toast to our progress and our aching muscles. That refreshment was to be the only supper I got that night because of a terrible mistake I made after we unpacked the horses.

I had been warned that Frances's bay gelding had no respect for hobbles. In fact, the story was that the agile little devil had won several horse races with hobbles on, much to the amazement of many poorer and wiser gamblers. The horse had equal contempt for picket ropes, but throwing advice aside, I tied the bay by a front foot to a large log. I believed he would be content to feed and rest after the long trip. Bob's two horses were belled, hobbled, and turned loose.

We hadn't been in camp ten minutes when Smokey and the big sorrel hopped a stone's throw away from camp looking for grass. The bay gelding took it in his head that he was going to join them and took off at a run. He had enough length in his picket rope to be at full speed when the slack snapped out of the rope. I watched in helpless horror, thinking I was about to witness the horse break his leg. The log he was tied to never budged, and the horse did a complete somersault before the rope gave a loud pop. The bay, never losing momentum, rolled onto his feet at a fast run. I got the feeling that horse had used the same trick several times before and actually enjoyed it.

Smokey saw the bay speeding toward him and decided a horse race was in progress. Being the kind of horse who hates second place, Smokey broke into a rough, hobbled lope behind the thundering bay. The big sorrel wasn't sure what the excitement was all about, but was determined not to be left out of the picture. He joined the get-away, despite his hobbles, as the other two horses started for the back trail. Bob and I each grabbed a halter and lead rope and set out in pursuit of the homeward-bound horses. I had a temporary lapse of humor and cussed everything I could think of—mostly myself for underestimating the ornery little bay.

The horses disappeared over a saddle in the ridge above camp with us far behind. By the time Bob and I puffed our way to the crest of the saddle, it was dark. We paused and listened intently in the quiet evening. Occasionally, we heard a distant bell of the still-traveling horses.

Finally, I said to Bob, "Why don't you go back to camp for tonight? In the morning, ask Frances to keep an eye on camp, grab enough food for both of us, and start following horses tracks. I'll keep following the horses tonight and try to head them off. There's no telling where or when the knot-heads will stop."

"OK," he said, handing me the halter and lead rope he was carrying. "Good luck."

I may have seen darker nights, but I couldn't remember one. I was so tired, I lost all sense of time. After what was probably a couple of hours but seemed like a couple of days, I suddenly heard horses bells a few hundred feet in front of me. I approached the grazing horses carefully, caught Smokey and the bay, then unhobbled the big sorrel.

The return to camp seemed even blacker than before. Thick clouds moved low overhead. Adding to the spirit of the evening, I successfully soaked both legs to the knees while crossing a small stream. I thought about riding one of the horses bareback but was aching so badly I decided riding would be more painful than walking. Also, if the horse dumped me, I was absolutely certain I would shatter into a thousand, miserable, tiny pieces. When I finally reached camp, I tied the horses high and short and laid my bedroll on a remarkably rough piece of real estate. Bob's voice came out of a pile of saddle pads, bedroll, and tarps.

"Appears you recovered our losses."

"Yeah," was all I could reply.

Little did I know that the night's fun was not over.

Just as I laid my head on my rolled jacket, it began to rain on my exposed down sleeping bag. I was too tired to do more than laugh at my misfortune, pull my jacket over my head, and fall asleep.

An hour later as the eastern sky glowed, I woke up shivering. The ground was white with ice and snow and a biting wind blew hard. Water was running under my wet bedroll, soaking my hips in a puddle of slush. I decided I could either lie there a few more minutes and freeze to death or get up and recover life. I pulled my wet denim jacket over the wet clothes I had slept in. With shaking hands, I built a fire that was much more than a token symbol of camping; it was a matter of survival.

Bob's head poked out of his mound of dry bedroll and tarps, sized up the situation, and jokingly asked if breakfast was ready.

"You know, there's nothing like a stroll in the mountains and a good night's rest to make ya feel like a million bucks," I chattered between clenched teeth.

We finally made it to camp that day, despite Bob being attacked by an angry mamma moose. He claimed his life was saved by his amazing feat of hiding beneath the backpack he was wearing after he dove into a convenient clump of willows. In a moment after his disappearing act, the protective mother moose retreated into the brush to find her calf.

What a camp we had! Down from the timberline nearly 2,000 feet, it was heaven on earth. We pitched the tent among towering lodgepole pines near a milk-blue glacial stream. Shadows of nearly invisible cutthroat trout moved slowly across the gravel bottoms of deep pools. The horses grazed on lush grass amid tall yellow-leafed willows. A duck and her long line of nearly-grown ducklings occasionally could be seen in a nearby slough. One evening, the dark shape of a tremendous beaver silently swam up the rushing stream. Sheltering our meadow were the magnificent mountains that seemed to touch the fast-moving clouds in the deep blue sky. We were rich beyond description in that world not yet developed, improved, refined, commercialized, modernized, and civilized by man.

We decided not to hunt on the first day of sheep season. Instead, we enjoyed our wonderful camp and recovered from the exhausting journey. Later that afternoon, we wanted to catch some fish for supper. Bob and Frances fished upstream while I tried my luck near camp. After three casts failed to catch a fish, I switched priorities. I nestled down on a sunny, sandy beach and fell fast asleep.

The following morning, we got down to the brass tacks of sheep hunting. The three of us arose early, ate breakfast, packed lunches, and started hiking up a well-used game trail toward timberline. It was a beautiful day. Although we moved along steadily, we didn't reach sheep country until midday. We traveled along several miles of grassy mountain slopes far above timberline while glassing every possible spot that might conceal a sheep. Our destination was a large basin where I had often seen rams in previous years. We arrived at the basin late in the afternoon and had only enough time to give it a quick glassing before it was time to return to camp. I had a gut feeling the basin had not revealed all it contained. We decided that Bob and I would return to the basin the following day with a backpack camp and hunt the area for several days. Frances—who was not a hunter and had mixed emotions about it— volunteered to care for the horses at our base camp. We arrived back at camp and had a pleasant moonlight supper beside the rushing stream.

The next morning, Bob and I strapped on our backpacks and started up the mountain. Our spirits had the easy job of carrying our hearts skyward while our legs had the more difficult task of carrying our bodies and heavy packs up the mountain. We rested among brightly colored flowers beside a small brook.

We reached the basin in good time. There were several hours of daylight remaining when we removed our packs and eased out onto an observation point. I immediately spotted two rams below us. Both were half-curls bedded down below some huge boulders. We glassed and glassed for other rams but could find no more with the two young rams. In a while, Bob left to search a part of the basin we couldn't see from our position.

I continued to look for sheep until the two bedded half-curls got to their feet and began to graze. I glassed along the rim to see if I could locate Bob. Suddenly, I saw him a thousand yards away, and he was frantically waving for me to join him!

I nearly flew over the neck-breaking terrain. I knew he had spotted sheep. The questions were: How many? How big? Where at? When I reached him, we crawled behind a pile of large rocks on the edge of the basin. Bob pointed to a small patch of grass halfway down the steep wall. I focused the spotting scope on four bedded rams. Two were half-curls and the other two had horns well past the three-quarter-curl mark. Time was running short as the sun approached the western horizon.

The brisk wind was suitable for Bob to conceal himself behind a long rock outcropping and descend to the level of the rams. Even so, it looked as if he would be forced to take a long shot. I was to stay where I was and keep an eye on things from above. Bob hid behind the outcropping and started down the steep slope, using the classic inch-worm, rump-slide stalk—feet, butt, hands, feet, butt, hands. He was nearly halfway there when the rams decided to move. Bob froze while the rams grazed. The two largest rams playfully butted heads before again lying down. I used hand signals to make sure Bob knew the position of the largest ram. He slowly nodded in agreement.

A short time later, he was as close as possible to the rams, perhaps three hundred yards. It was not a ridiculous range for a good marksman, but far enough to dictate calm, deliberate shooting. Bob found a suitable rock rest, laid his rifle on his folded jacket, and paused to collect himself. Just at that moment, a gale of swirling wind hit him and flapped the arm of his jacket like a bird's wing. I couldn't believe my eyes and quickly glassed the rams. None had caught the movement. It was almost more than I could stand. Bob regained control of the situation and again paused to steady his nerves. He glanced at me, and I gave him the thumbs-up sign. The moment of truth had arrived.

The largest ram faced slightly uphill to Bob and gave him a quartering shot at the shoulder. Holding a bit too high, the first bullet nicked the big ram's horn before clipping the hair on the top of his spine. The ram jumped to his feet and shook his head like he had just taken a barroom-brawl blow to the temple. The ram spun just as Bob fired his second round and I saw dust fly from the rocks behind the sheep. The rams, not sure where the shots had come from, ran toward Bob. On the third shot, I thought I saw the largest ram flinch slightly, but he continued to run through the loose rock like a racehorse. We lost sight of the running rams for a second before the largest ram and the two half-curls suddenly burst into view a short distance below Bob.

They disappeared into a deep ravine before Bob could fire a shot. The smaller legal, three-quarter-curl ram jumped up on a rock slab twenty-five yards below Bob and stood looking around.

"Should I take him?" he called to me.

"No!," I screamed down at him, "I think you may have hit the big one."

Bob and the ram stared at each other for a few seconds before the animal raced away, following the others. There was a suspenseful silence as Bob walked down to where the rams had passed.

Suddenly, he spun around and yelled, "Blood! Lung blood! Lots of it!"

I glassed the bottom of the basin where the rams had headed. Three rams suddenly appeared. I watched them until they ran out of sight and looked for a fourth ram lagging behind, but none appeared. Bob walked over to the deep ravine.

"Here he is! Dead!," Bob shouted.

It's hard to describe how rough and rocky the basin was where Bob had shot the ram. We risked breaking our necks while cautiously walking over the same talus slopes the sheep had crossed at a hard run. When we thought of the way they had skimmed over that rough terrain, we were struck with awe and respect for their ability.

It was nearly dark by the time we finished caping and gutting the ram. Finding a level spot to camp proved to be an impossible task. We finally rolled our sleeping bags out on a small, grassy slope, too small for the two of us. An exceptionally hard rock prevented me from rolling down the hill and I, in turn, propped Bob in place on the grassy spot. One of my knees was throbbing as if someone had hit the kneecap with a hammer. I figured the pain was from a torn or stretched ligament but could do nothing for it at the time. We spent a restless, though absolutely windless and moonlit night, counting the stars.

We were up early the next morning and finished breakfast before the first ray of sunlight hit the top of the rugged mountains around us. We could easily understand why sheep would want to live in such a beautiful place, but we marveled at their ability to survive in so harsh a climate and such rough terrain.

We planned to pack the camp and sheep down to timberline, return to base camp with only our bedrolls, and finish packing the ram to base camp with the horses. Packing the ram to timberline proved to be painful. My knee was worse, and it was quite painful to bend it. While balancing two sheep hindquarters on his shoulders with his hands, Bob stepped out on an icy snow field. Instantly, both of his feet flew straight out in front of his face. In that position and without the use of his hands to break the fall, he crashed heavily onto the ice. For quite a while, he lay there silent. Only later, after I saw that he hurt too much to catch me, did I laugh. He was OK—still able to pack the ram.

We finished shuttling the camp and ram to timberline at about noon and immediately started for base camp. While crossing a rockslide, I stepped on a teetering, washtub-sized rock. Because of my injured knee, I couldn't jump out of the way as it rolled. I nearly blacked out as the rock came to rest on my foot. Luckily, nothing was broken and, after a rest, I was ready to continue. It was now Bob's turn to laugh. He asked me if I wanted him to shoot me and put me out of my misery. We started walking again, the pain in my throbbing knee competing with the sharp pain in my foot.

Shortly before we arrived at base camp, we jumped a six-point bull elk from his bed in the heavy timber. His handsome white-tipped antlers rocked slightly as he trotted away. It was nearly dark when we dragged our weary bodies into base camp and collapsed on the ground.

"Frances," I pleaded, "this is an emergency, I tell ya. Please hand us the snake-bite bottle and fix us something to eat." She laughed and began her mission of mercy. When supper was finished, I gingerly laid back against a log, already more asleep than awake.

"Frances, you just saved my life," I mumbled.

"Do you think the world will hold that against me?," she asked innocently.

"Probably."

The following morning, I was elected to retrieve the ram with the horses while Bob and Frances gathered trout for supper.

I believe I was volunteered for my job when I explained how we could get the horse to where we had left the ram: "We can follow the Forest Service trail for a lot of the way before we have to pick our way cross-country. The trail stops at a big lake, but a horse like Smokey will slide off the rocks and into the water with no problem. Just take a dally with the lead rope and jerk the packhorse into the water when Smokey jumps in."

Actually I didn't mind retrieving the ram and cheerfully saddled Smokey and the big sorrel. During the long ride to the ram, I had the inexplicable feeling I would see more sheep that day. I constantly watched for signs of game. I was riding through wind-stunted trees at timberline just before I reached Bob's ram when, suddenly, Smokey stopped and stared ahead.

A band of rams burst from the trees a hundred yards in front of me. I caught glimpses of several curling horns and white rumps before they vanished. I quickly rode ahead to see if I could spot them again. A half-curl stood below a pile of huge, house-sized boulders. He stared at me with a puzzled look on his face, then leaped up on the rocks. The slick granite was too steep for him to walk on, and he was forced to jump off when he lost his balance. He stared at me again and looked somewhat embarrassed; it was beneath his dignity to have fouled up his getaway. The ram then took two long leaps and again sprang upon the rocks. Instead of slowing to a walk, he kept his momentum by leaping and springing up the jumbled rocks. The sure-footed animal zigzagged and bounced off the rocks like a rubber ball, ricocheting up the granite with perfect timing, grace, and strength. It was one of the most amazing feats I have ever seen an animal perform.

The young ram paused at the top of the boulder pile and looked down at me as if to say, "That was easy; now let's see you do it." Then he spun around and followed the other rams while I sat on the horse and shook my head in disbelief.

The excitement was not over for the day. It was mid-afternoon by the time I loaded the backpack camp and the ram on the big sorrel. On the way back to base camp, I took the horses up a very steep elk trail in order to climb above a cliff. It was there that the sorrel made a slip on slick rock and lost his balance. He nearly went over backward, then turned downhill to try to catch himself. The horse made a few short, skidding hops before stopping on the very edge of the cliff. One more hop would have spread horse flesh, tack, camping gear, and sheep horns all over the landscape. I bailed from Smokey and grabbed the lead rope of the quivering sorrel. I steadied him until he stopped shaking, then led him back from the drop-off. I was still thanking my lucky stars when I rode into camp a few hours later.

To her credit and my delight, Frances made an absolutely wonderful meal that evening. The entire supper revolved around juicy sheep meat and fresh trout. We planned to pack out of the mountains in a few days and had no reason to spare the groceries. We feasted like royalty.

In a few days, we would walk out of the timeless mountains and return to the world of clocks.

Chapter Ten
A Special Mountain

 January. The mountains and high plains were locked in a frozen grasp. The animals were miles to the south in warmer regions or deeply huddled in the insulating protection nature had given them. Only the fish, swimming indifferently under thick ice, were unaware of the penetrating cold. The wind, which at times wailed like a banshee across the land, was now silent—not even a cold whisper hissed in the frosted spruce tops. The plaintive chirps and flutterings of juncos were amplified into a startling clamor, shattering the eerie silence.

The bulky figure of a warmly dressed human knelt over the crisscrossed rawhide webbing of a pair of snowshoes and tugged at the bindings. Frost highlighted the wolf-hair ruff that rimmed the young man's parka hood, and his breath slowly rose in a sparkling vapor. On his back was a heavy pack containing the precious provisions he needed for two, perhaps three nights of camping.

Earlier, he had spooked a small herd of mule deer from a south-facing slope. An inquisitive forked-horn buck watched the intruder and stomped an impatient front hoof as if demanding to know the man's purpose and destination. Neither of those questions could be answered; there are times when a young man, free of spirit and sound of leg, travels for the sheer joy of being alive, alert, and invincible. A purpose is an excuse, a cover-up for the search for freedom. A destination only restricts his soul's yearning to explore.

In the heavy timber, the snow was deep and powdery. His rests were frequent as he labored to the high peaks above. Tracks told which animals knew the agony of moving through deep snow and which had the gift of buoyancy. The snowshoe rabbits, mice, ermine, and pine marten fared well; the grouse, fox, coyotes, and humans floundered, as best they could. Above timberline, wind-swept tracks of bighorn sheep and elk showed that they had learned to avoid the treacherous drifts, resigning themselves to the bitter gale winds of the alpine.

The man's pack and snowshoes were left in the shelter of the last weather-stunted trees at timberline. Using the same wind-swept routes of the hoofed animals, he climbed higher, intent on reaching the tallest peak before dark.

Near the top, the wind blew fiercely and lashed at bare skin with unrelenting cruelty. The man paused behind a rock for protection and studied the valley far below. The thin shadow of a trail across a small opening marked the place he had trudged hours before. Miles beyond, the waterways carved the valley floor into a maze of rolling hills and steep canyons. The land itself lay wrinkled and folded in disarray, the weathered skin of ancient Mother Earth. Millions of dots of sagebrush gave a mottled texture and color to the endless miles of snow.

In the center of the valley floor, a large mesa, miles across, stood in contrasting relief. Sweeping the mesa again with his binoculars, the young man noticed an out-of-place dark mass near its edge. The mass grew larger, sent a black tongue across the flat, white ground. The tongue became a winding stream like a black snake slithering on a carpet of white. From his distant perch, the man watched hundreds and hundreds of elk migrating—part of the great Yellowstone herd as they migrated to their winter range. The mass of elk, four and five abreast and nearly a mile long, slowly flowed across the mesa and disappeared over the far rim, leaving the man marveling at nature's mysteries.

I was the man, of course, and can still picture that incredible black line of elk, the largest herd of free-ranging animals I have ever seen. That place was a special spot on earth, and deserved a special spot in my heart. That is why, ten years later and 1,200 miles away, I became angry during a conversation with a stranger about that special place.

Meredith and I were on a winter vacation to Mexico. While traveling, we believe in taking our time to see new things and immerse ourselves in the local sights and culture. We drove our small pickup with camper, and left the sub-zero temperatures and drifting snow behind. We vowed not to slow down until we saw sandals and sunglasses. Not even the border country qualified that year. The customs official wore a coat in a drizzling rain and commented, "Mucho frio!"

We continued south. Near the southern end of the Mexican state of Sonora, we came to a small town near Alamos. Old folks sat visiting, young people strolled around the palm-tree-lined plaza, children played here and there, and brilliant flowers bloomed in abundance. We had arrived at our destination.

Through Meredith's survival Spanish and other bilingual people, we learned that a Mexican outfitter lived at the edge of town. Sensing that we had much in common and wishing to find out more about the hunting and fishing in Mexico, we bounced along cobblestone streets, heading for the outfitter's ranch. There we found an immaculate hacienda, brilliant white stucco under red tile roofs, and blooming poinsettia bushes more than eight feet tall. The outfitter, polite and sincere, was a perfect host and spoke English well. We made arrangements with him to camp near his orchards before visiting with him about his operation. He explained that his father had built the ranch years ago, and it was still run as a Brahma cattle ranch, truck farm, summer resort, and headquarters for winter dove and quail hunting. I couldn't help comparing the setup with many dude ranches of the western United States.

Our host's most obvious virtue was his unequaled ability to mix the strongest margarita in Mexico. He invited us into his lodge for cocktails following the afternoon hunt, introduced us to some of his American dove-hunting guests, and handed us each a glass of his special recipe, containing more inert energy than an equal volume of nitroglycerine. The outfitter filled us in on Mexican game laws, of which there seemed to be few, and the country's hunting and fishing opportunities, which seemed to be great, before he excused himself to attend to some ranch business.

Meredith and I continued to visit with a couple of good ol' boys from Texas and talked of the day's dove shooting south of the border. In a short time, another American guest, a middle-aged man with a constant cocky smile on his face, entered the room and joined our group. The man was accompanied by a fairly attractive young lady whom he introduced as his secretary. His boastful expression and voice told us that "secretary" was an euphemism. It was clear the man had brought forbidden fruit with him on his Mexican dove shoot, and the secretary was somewhat embarrassed to be introduced as such.

The man rubbed me the wrong way when he spoke of the dozens and dozens of doves he had shot that day for no other reason than to see them die. Nor did he gain any respect from me when he voiced arrogant estimations of the outfitter's employees. The man had less respect for the young people who retrieved the dead doves than he would have had for the bird dogs they replaced. He spoke of the women who cleaned the kill in exchange for a portion of the dove breasts as little more than slaves at his disposal. The epitome of arrogance finally won the prize with me after he asked where I lived and hunted.

He explained he was familiar with the area after spotting a huge bighorn ram during the winter months from his small airplane, landing at the nearest airport, driving a rented car back to the area, and trying to poach the ram. When he finally got to the top of the mountain, the man said—adding emphasis with expletives—the ram wasn't there.

I was more than perturbed to think I had traveled all that distance only to find a despicable slob who attempted to poach the same sheep I hunted religiously each fall. Caught up in his own boasting and self-importance, he failed to realize how deeply he insulted me by desecrating the very mountain where I had stood ten years before watching the long, black line of elk. It cut me to the quick to hear the slob speak so disrespectfully about the wildlife and wildlands I loved.

From that point on, my end of the conversation slumped while I contemplated the consequences of telling the poacher what I thought of him. Prudence and the thought of foreign jails helped me to regain my composure.

A glance at my wife told me that she, too, was losing her bout with the potent margarita and her patience with the poacher. Knowing a second round of the drink would put us both on our hands and knees, we politely excused ourselves and bid "buenas nochés" to the others.

If there is any justice in the world, the poacher we met in Mexico someday will feel the long arm of the law and, from a certain mountain, bighorn rams will stare down on a flat mesa in a snow-covered valley and watch a long, dark mass of migrating elk. In spirit, I will be with those rams, each year, until the end of time.

Chapter Eleven
Therapy Stream

 I have learned that there is much more involved with hunting and fishing than just going afield a couple of weekends in search of meat, sport, or recreation. Certainly much more is required of hunters than merely banging away at a mallard drake or a buck antelope once a year. It has become clear that wildlife needs our attention every day. This resource cannot be forgotten and ignored after the freezer is packed full of winter's meat and the rifles are put away.

"The price of liberty is vigilance," a great statesman once said. Likewise, I have come to understand that the price of a healthy wildlife resource is vigilance as well.

Wildlife's and wildland's cause has a long history that has taken many forms. The seeds of the vigil were planted many generations ago. From the eighteenth century, a few far-sighted leaders realized as our young nation was altering the face of the continent to develop a civilization that our nation also needed to retain lands for wildlife habitat. Those people recognized that with no wildlands, there could be no wildlife and, with that, the conservation of wildlife began.

The vigil continues today. Caring people who possess a love and commitment to nature, carry on the legacy of North American wildlife conservation. Several years ago, I enlisted in the conservation cause to protect and promote our wildlife and wildland heritage. I have tried to serve my time on the wildlife vigil and repay to the resource all of the things it has given me. I have served in volunteer organizations, helped with wildlife fund raisers, worked with wildlife managers, and talked with my lawmakers. During several years of conservation involvement, I learned the true commitment this cause requires. It is grueling, endless, and critical work. The rewards come with the sight of a wedge of geese silhouetted against a red sunset, the thrill of hearing bugling elk, or the satisfaction of lifting a trout from pure, clean mountain streams.

A few years ago, I had a particularly discouraging encounter with a group of folks who would pave the last acre of wetlands in order to build another gas station and who embrace the notion that the only good tree is a tree on logging

73

truck racing for the nearest mill. I was worn. I can only talk to a fence post for so long before I realize I am wasting my time.

I was feeling fairly low in spirits following that encounter and packed into the mountains by myself to fish. As my saddle and packhorses climbed and puffed, I thought about how easy it would be to just hunt and fish—to let someone else worry about habitat, and to forget about the next generation of hunters and anglers.

I camped for several days and fished one of the most spectacular, pristine streams I had ever seen. The stream was perhaps twenty five feet wide and complemented perfectly the towering and jagged peaks from which it flowed. Huge glaciers a dozen miles above my camp were the source of its water. The slower water and deep pools below countless foaming, frothing rapids were shades of turquoise. Glacial milk deposited white sand along the stream bed in which the pale native cutthroat trout were camouflaged. Dippers fluttering to their nests on the stream's sides passed over bright green moss beds watered by the constant spray of the cascade's mist. Moose and coyote tracks mixed on sandbars. It was not a bad place to spend some time—working the eddies and pools and healing the mind and spirit while exercising the body.

The timing of my fishing trip was good. It was mid-August and numbers of bugs had peaked. One to three pound cutthroats responded to my fisheries inventory by devouring the flies I offered.

Most anglers have had the kind of day when everything is absolutely perfect, when the rod in their hands works magic upon the water, and many hours of ecstasy elapse before they release their last fish and return to earth. The hours spent away from the world's rat race and engrossed in the world where life flows calmly and harmoniously are hours that heal. The soothing rush of water over rocks, the satisfaction of placing a fly perfectly at the head of a deep pool, and the rush of life into the veins while holding a bent and jumping rod, relieve the stress and worry to lighten life's burdens.

The contests along the stream that day were not all one-sided. Besides rejuvenation, the stream also gave me a fish-that-got-away story, making my experience complete. On the bank, several trees leaned well over the water. At their foot, two limby snags laid on the stream surface. In mid-stream behind the two snags, I saw the waving outline of a large cutthroat. The fish was much larger than any I had seen that day, as long as my forearm from elbow to fingertips. The depth and heaviness of the trout's outline hinted of the powerful fight that would be required to bring it to the bank. I dearly wanted to hook that fish, but try as I might to cast a fly to it, I could not avoid the overhanging trees.

Perhaps a more skillful person could have correctly placed a fly. Perhaps it just was not meant to be. Perhaps the lesson that many things in life often lay just beyond our reach and capability was a lesson more important than the experience of hooking the fish.

I'm not sure how many fish I worked to the bank to release that day. It may have been a dozen or it may have been many dozens. Regardless, it was enough to mend my worn resolve. When the afternoon shadows of the forest stretched across the water, I made a last cast, released a last fish, and started walking for camp. At peace. Optimistic. Complete.

Chapter Twelve
Adventures On The Wing

 When I was younger, I thought of the Rocky Mountain states as a big-game hunter's paradise with elk-filled meadows, mule deer with towering racks, mountain goats perched on knife-edged ridges, bighorn rams clashing heads, and pronghorns racing with the wind over endless prairies. I also discovered the excitement of feisty, rod-bending trout as they danced across crystal-clear water. For years, though, I overlooked the enjoyment of bird hunting and robbed myself of much pleasure.

Birds in the mountain states? Not many, but enough, I discovered, to make it worthwhile to tromp the autumn fields in search of upland and migratory birds. I realize the most exciting days of pheasant hunting I have had would bore a South Dakota hunter. I have been laughed at by East Coast goose hunters when I excitedly told them about flocks of a few dozen honkers slicing the sky with perfect vees. The sight of jumping a few ducks off a cottonwood-lined stream can't compare to watching clouds of birds fly past blinds along the major flyways. Still, I have had my special moments, moments often summoned from the storage vaults of my memory and fondly relived.

After winter's meat is in the freezer, when the mountains are white and the big-game herds are trickling onto their winter ranges, there is nothing I love more than to stretch the fall hunting season out a few more days by strolling with a shotgun in hand through fields of yellow stalks and sloughs of golden stems.

❧

Dawn. Morning was a white arc above the eastern horizon, slowly flowing over a flawless, star-speckled, black sky. I crawled partially out of my down bedroll, propped myself up on one elbow, and raked the embers of the campfire with a short stick until tiny, red coals lay exposed and glowing. I laid sun-dried grass on the embers, carefully arranged small sticks and, finally, placed limbs from a beaver-felled cottonwood on the smoking pile of kindling. This task finished, I hurriedly burrowed back into the depths of my bedroll.

Lying on my back, I watched the miracle of a new day beginning. Waves gently lapped at the shore of the small lake beside the camp, repeatedly washing the small stones at the water's edge. To the east, the white arc continued to climb and grow in size. Suddenly the frantic, whistling noise of fast-moving wings told of an early flight of ducks circling the perimeter of the lake. The clamor of alarmed Canada geese arose from the depths of a cattail marsh across the lake, betraying the bird's presence and location. The excited chorus of geese was followed by the loud quacking of a mallard hen as she flapped into the air. Then peaceful silence again reigned over the morning.

The smoldering fire ignited into flames, throwing a circle of light on the small campsite and signaling that it was time for me to get up. Across the fire, I looked to see if my bird-hunting partner was awake. The only sign of life from him was heavy, slow breathing from under a mound of bedroll. Lying against my partner's back was an enormous black labrador; his bearlike head rose and curiously followed my every movement. An old, soiled hunting coat, cherished and priceless, lay draped over the dog's hindquarters. Several elastic shotshell loops above the coat's pockets were vacant, hinting of the previous day's successful hunt.

I dressed each part of my anatomy in the order it emerged from the warm bedroll: hat, shirt, vest, coat, longjohns, pants, socks, and boots. A piece of homemade deer jerky served as breakfast. I reached for my featherweight 20-gauge, and the lab's tail began to thump heavily. A whispered but firm "Stay!" command stopped the tail-thumping—and completely broke the dog's heart.

There are times when I want, and need, to hunt alone—only me, a straight-shooting gun, and a place to ramble freely while following nothing but my own whims and instincts. I walked alone from camp with the sweetheart 20-gauge cradled in my arms.

The white arc of dawn had changed to rose, then orange. The cloud in the northwest sky was rimmed with red. A coot flapped across the surface of the lake, suddenly folded its wings, and plowed to an abrupt halt in the mercurial, molten reflection of dawn. I skirted the water's edge, following raccoon tracks locked in the stiff, frosted mud. A steady whoosh, whoosh, whoosh came from overhead. With its head drawn against its body, a blue heron flapped lazily into the east.

Turning from the lake, I climbed a slight rise to a saddle between low hills and descended the other side. There, a small creek fed by irrigation run-off meandered through a valley of tall grasses, chest-high weed patches, red willows, and thorny windbreaks of Russian olive trees. During the previous day, several brilliantly colored rooster pheasants had fallen before our guns along the stream. Perhaps I would be lucky again. Maybe the tall grasses of the valley would yield another bird. At any step, a cackling blur of color could explode from beneath my feet. Cautiously, I waded into the cover.

Tory Taylor doing what he loves best—exploring new country from the back of a horse.

Pausing beside the creek, an amoeba-like line of geese rose from a distant reservoir and flapped their way to the nearby farmlands. Dry stems and weed stalks crunched under my boots. Reaction jerked the light 20-gauge nearly to my shoulder before my brain interpreted the frantic running noise to my left. I lowered the gun even before the rabbit was out of sight, as my thoughts signaled cottontail, not pheasant. I spent a moment standing quietly to let my pounding heart return to a moderate pace.

I slowly zig-zagged toward the tip of a finger of knee-deep weeds and grass. A short, faint, unaccountable rustling noise came from five paces in front of me. I froze for a full ten seconds, then moved a step forward. Instantly, from two feet ahead of my boot laces, a brown flash shot skyward, the fast, beating wings shattering the quiet morning. At the same instant, another hen pheasant rocketed from behind me.

The 20-gauge was up and I heard myself softly saying, "Come on rooster, come on." He came up twenty feet in front of me and was already well into the air before I saw the dark emerald head, the distinct white collar, the copper breast, and the long tail feathers following a blur of gray wings. It was an easy shot; the rooster folded and fell heavily into shallow grass, tips of tail feathers sticking out from the yellow stems marking the spot.

I again cradled the 20-gauge in my arms, faced the rising sun, and basked my body in the blinding rays, my soul in the glory of a golden morning.

❦

November. Old Man Winter had covered the world with a biting, burning white. The heater in my four-wheel-drive pickup was on high as I broke trail down miles of snow-filled country lanes. Bird season was in full swing and I was looking for anything that flapped, fluttered, or flew. One chukar lay on the floor mat of the passenger's side where I hoped it would remain thawed until I could clean it in the relative warmth of my shop at home.

The only open waters remaining after many nights of frigid temperatures were the warm-water irrigation drains and occasional inlets of ponds and reservoirs. From a high bench overlooking a small reservoir, I used binoculars to inspect the frosty world below. Acres of cattail marshes met the upper end of the reservoir, the only open water being a black, oblong hole where a spring fed the reservoir near the edge of the cattails. The dark opening of water, perhaps fifty feet long, stood out in sharp contrast to the ice covering the remainder of the reservoir. It looked even larger with the rows and rows of mallard ducks sitting in a solid ring around the water's edge. The open water literally could contain no more ducks, and the ring of birds on the edge, four to six feet wide, was equally packed. The flock included both local and migrating northern birds already pushed south by the freeze-up.

I glassed the flock for ten minutes, listening to the various quacks and calls penetrate the cold, still air. Finally, the frigid air snapped me out of my trance. I made my way down a deep ravine, heading for the distance black oval of birds.

A hundred yards from the ducks, I found myself floundering in the head-high cattails protruding from an alarmingly thin layer of ice. Fluffy cattail seeds were in my eyes, in my mouth, and stuck to my runny nose. Although the cattails snapped loudly, they were no match for the commotion of the quacking, splashing, flapping ducks. When the tall cover dwindled to knee-high islands of cattails, I inched ahead on hands and knees. Once, the thin, crystal-clear ice cracked under my weight. I weighed the worth of the ducks compared to a dunking in the knee-deep water before again easing ahead.

Pausing near the ducks, I watched a muskrat swim under me through the glass-like ice. I finally reached a curtain of cattails and crouched ten yards from the edge of the swarm of mallards, a living carpet of bobbing heads. A dozen more ducks sailed into the mass on set wings, colliding with others during their landings. They whooshed barely over my head. My moment had arrived, but

I hesitated to stand. The sight and situation overwhelmed me. Here was a scene I might never witness again. Hoping to find a bird or two for the table, I had come face to face with hundreds of them.

Finally, I stood amid the loud quacking and splashing and, for a moment, every duck remained stunned, motionless, perfectly silent. Then, in unison, an incredible wave of ducks erupted into the sky. The roar of wings was deafening, almost like the roar of a waterfall. The whirling wind from their wings fanned my face. A second wave of ducks lifted from the ice and water, mallards so thick they could not all fly at once. A steady stream of stragglers followed like the tapering tail of a feathered comet. Overhead, the sky shown only as flashes of blue behind a kaleidoscope of beating wings.

Overwhelmed by it all, I was slow to choose a target. A large drake was one of the last to leave the water; my first shot somersaulted the duck onto the ice. Another drake climbed in a corkscrew pattern. My second shot knocked feathers off him and caused him to hover in the air. The final shot dropped the drake into the cattails at my side. The roar of wings loudly echoed in my ears. I turned to watch the unbelievable cloud of birds fly away. Already, ducks were peeling from the cloud—a small bunch here, a pair there—to search for other resting or feeding areas. A moment later, the last tiny specks disappeared over the horizon, and I was alone once more in a frozen, white world.

❦

December. Winter had arrived, bringing ducks and geese from the northern nesting grounds. Refusing to allow the drifting snow and icy winds to keep me indoors, I pulled on layer after layer of clothing, hung a set of binoculars around my neck, and picked up a pump-action 12-gauge. I had noticed small groups of mallards and goldeneyes along the nearby river and drooled when I thought of the sweet, rich fat melted on a baked duck.

It was a losing battle trying to ignore the icy blasts of snow in my face and the painful throb of cold in my feet as I inched along the cottonwood-covered banks. A pair of water ouzels dipped happily in water lined with delicate ice. I pushed through a tangle of willows and noticed movement on the opposite bank. Bouncing through a cottonwood grove were two mule-deer bucks—one a forked-horn, the other a large four-point. Deer season was open, but these two were safe. The shotgun in my hands showed it was birds, not deer, that I searched for. I watched the running deer through my binoculars until they disappeared up a sagebrush and juniper canyon.

It was a mistake to keep my mind on the deer as I again set out. I carelessly took three steps forward and a dozen mallards exploded into the air just out of shotgun range.

Feeling rather foolish, I happened to look at a snow-covered ice shelf at the water's edge. There, I noticed recent tracks and droppings of a river otter, a beautiful animal seldom seen in this area anymore. Staring into a small pool behind a table-sized rock, I saw the dark, waving outline of a large trout. Again, I realized my shotgun was not the tool I needed just then. The more I thought about the situation, the more I saw the comedy and beauty of it.

The cold began to burn my face and feet. I left the river and started for home without having fired a shot—no duck, no deer, no fish, nor even an otter sighting. Yet I felt lucky, very lucky, to know a place still existed on earth that offers such variety.

Chapter Thirteen
Elk Hunting at its Best

 There are elk hunts, and then there are elk hunts. This elk hunt was so textbook perfect that I cannot really think of how it could have been improved.

It was fairly late in the hunting season; the highcountry on the Buffalo Fork south of Yellowstone National Park was blanketed in white. During the weeks that had passed since the opening day of elk season, most hunters had gone home, snow had fallen several times, and many elk were starting to gather into large groups to migrate to lower elevations in Jackson Hole. All four of us—Duane, Burke, Eric, and I—wanted to put elk steaks into our freezers.

Leading eight packhorses behind our four saddlehorses, we made our way to elk camp, deep in the mountains, far into the quiet corners of a pristine wilderness where elk are kings and humans are transient visitors. The twelve horses traveled like a slow-moving snake up the winding, snowpacked trail.

Duane led the way. This quiet, gray-haired, willow-straight and willow-tough man was a veteran of many wilderness elk hunts. Like myself, he lives in the Rockies because of the wildlife they harbor and the wildlands which still remain. We share a reverence of horses and love nothing more than to explore new, untamed country from the back of a good horse. Just before we arrived at camp, Duane turned his horses off of the trail and, leaning over, stared down at the fresh snow beside him. As the rest of us approached, we copied Duane and saw the very distinct and very fresh tracks of a grizzly sow and cubs. Later, at camp, we lashed an extra bear pole high between two towering trees. From the poles we religiously hung all of our food, horse feed, and bear attractants. We didn't wish to offer mamma bear an opportunity to teach her cubs about raiding human camps, a lesson that ultimately leads to dead marauding bears.

Perhaps the greatest pleasure and satisfaction of this camp was how smoothly it ran. The four of us were seasoned hunters and campers. No one was burdened with all of the decisions or work, nor was anyone pampered or idle. Instead, we pitched in equally when anything was needed. If a meal needed cooked, it was soon simmering on the tin cook stove. If it was time to feed and check the horses, it was done. If the wood pile seemed in need of attention, then hand saws and axes were put to use. Our well-supplied camp contained every necessary tool and piece of camp gear for elk hunting, and every item was neatly in its place. This spirit and situation made it possible to devote most of our time to hunting.

After several morning and evening hunts, we came to some conclusions. It was soon clear to us that we were the only hunters camped in the area and that there were large concentrations of elk, deer, and moose here as well. We also concluded that the heavy crust of snow that crunched loudly underfoot was going to make hunting more difficult. In addition, we felt that, with our snug camp, generous food supply, and adequate horse feed, we really did not care if it took extra time to fill some hunting tags. We had come to enjoy ourselves while hunting and that simply could not be rushed.

I was the first to kill an elk. Leaving camp a few hours before sunset, I walked to a south-facing, timbered slope. At the bottom of the slope, the timber was broken with small openings and aspen groves. Further up the slope, it became increasingly steeper with larger openings as it approached timberline. It was useless trying to follow tracks. Elk, deer, and moose tracks were so numerous and intertwined that following a single trail was impossible.

I had crunched my way through the noisy snow toward the edge of a steep ravine. Shielded by an island of timber on my right, a cow elk suddenly barked from several hundred yards away. The commotion from her deep, chesty barks seemed loud enough to travel for miles. I was caught flat footed, but hoped for the best as I chambered a round and eased toward the cow.

As I approached the far side of the island of trees, I caught glimpses of the cow. She was above me on the very edge of a rim rock and continued to bark a warning of my approach. Just as I finally reached an opening in the trees where I could seriously consider putting an end to the noisy barking with my rifle, the cow spun and disappeared beyond the edge of the rim rock.

The cow then angled uphill. I knew my best chance, though slim, was to climb and try to parallel the elk. There was no reason to attempt to be quiet and the pace I set soon had me bellowing for air. Occasionally, I heard the cow bark and saw flashes of other elk as they climbed through wind-stunted trees. I puffed through a strip of trees and came to a bowl at the head of a steep draw. The top edge of the bowl was perhaps a half mile above me and was dotted with patches of trees in large openings. Everywhere in those openings were elk.

I had walked into well over a hundred and fifty head of browsing and alerted elk, all seeming to have their eyes and ears turned in my direction. Singles and small bunches began moving slowly away from me and working their way further toward the head of the ravine. Several small bulls bugled while cows and calves talked back and forth.

Not quite two hundred yards straight above me at the top of a very steep, snow-covered hillside, a line of elk filed from the timber. I steadied my rifle against a large pine and studied the situation. What appeared to be a dry cow was last in the line of elk. She and several other elk paused on the top of a four-foot-tall rock ledge and stared down at me. Not wishing to fight my way uphill in the deep snow any longer, I suddenly had an idea—break the cow's neck and let gravity bring my winter's meat to me instead of having to climb to a dead elk.

I set my scope's crosshairs on the cow's neck, just ahead of the point of her shoulder and, just as she started to turn her head away from me, I squeezed the trigger. Through the scope, I saw the cow's head flip violently around just before she fell from the rock ledge and slid toward me as if I was reeling her in on a fishing line. The cow slid, rolled, and finally stopped less than twenty yards from the tree I had used as a rest. It was the best shot I ever made at an elk. The entire time I gutted the cow, I could still see and hear the elk herd. I cheerfully walked to camp before dark and started the evening meal while waiting for the others to return from their hunts.

The cow I shot seemed to break the ice. The following morning, as I saddled a riding horse and two packhorses to retrieve the cow I had killed the evening before, two rifle shots, spaced a minute apart, echoed from below camp. Burke and Duane had discovered a large herd of elk grazing in a huge, open meadow and had stalked the wary herd from two separate routes. Burke carefully worked his way to within easy rifle range before shooting an elk. Duane, who was several hundred yards away from the herd when Burke shot and spooked the herd, tried a long shot at a standing, isolated cow. His shot fell short. Later, when Duane paced the distance he had shot, he realized the elk had been much further than he had estimated.

On my way to pack my elk to camp, I rode past Burke and Duane just as they finished gutting Burke's cow. I was on an Appaloosa gelding with a no-nonsense, serious disposition. One of the packhorses I led was a four-year-old gelding, a huge horse with some draft-horse ancestry. On Mother's Day four years earlier, I had held this horse's head out of the corral dust as he was being brought into this world by one of my mares. My other packhorse was a small, snorty Morgan who had known several owners. Neither packhorse had ever carried an elk before. I wondered if my packing job might turn into a rodeo as I worked my horses up the mountain side to my elk.

My thoughts were suddenly interrupted by the muffled report of a rifle shot coming from the valley below me. I speculated about the rifle shot as I carefully, and successfully, loaded my elk quarters onto the rookie packhorses. Later, at camp, I learned that Eric also had filled his elk tag when a small group of elk ran past him. By the end of the day, we had three elk hanging at our camp.

Besides an elk tag, I also carried a deer license. With my priority purpose of elk hunting done, I now had the luxury of hunting for a deer. Numerous times during the hunt I could have killed a deer, but I was saving my tag for a special buck, the kind that hunters dream about often, but rarely ever see. I hunted several times looking for an old buck, spent many pleasant hours searching alone on beautiful mountain slopes and in dark, quiet forests. If a big buck was there, I never saw him.

One morning at daylight, Duane walked above camp on a horse trail and stopped instantly at the sight of a bull elk feeding a short distance away. In a flash, Duane's rifle was up, killing the bull with a single shot. Hearing but one rifle shot, we all correctly surmised that our elk hunting was finished.

A few days later, during our ride from the camp with our packhorses fully laden with meat and gear, I arranged the hunt in numerical terms. Four hunters. Twelve horses. Six days. Five shots. Four elk. One million happy memories. Those are the kind of figures I like!

Chapter Fourteen
Kansas Corn Fields and Corny Characters

 You must keep a careful watch on Kansas bird hunters. They are a crafty and fun-loving bunch. One fall, I journeyed to their state after receiving the most innocent invitation to join some of them for their annual bird hunt. The invitation was well-rehearsed. How smoothly and easily they hooked this wide-eyed, greenhorn with their honeyed stories of clouds of pheasants which, to hear them tell it, nearly blocked out the sun. How casually they retold accounts of swarming quail attacking grain fields like so many hungry locusts, devastating crops, and ruining farmers' dreams. How sincere they were in their reverence for a bird unknown to me called a prairie chicken, a bird worshipped for its supernatural powers of avoiding shotguns.

They talked of bird hunting superstars who, at some time in their lives, had actually smitten a prairie chicken and had instantly been placed on the tallest pedestals in the Bird Hunters' Hall of Fame.

Oh! I fell hook, line, and sinker for their solemn, straight-faced stories. They had plotted well. Knowing full well about snipes and jackalopes, I shamed myself by being such an easy target. Always, when placing the baiting stories in front of me, they would stand alone, unable to look anyone else in the eye. This should have tipped me off that something was amiss. I can only hope that they bruised each other's ribs with their pounding elbows when my back was turned to their muffled snickers.

The friendly town of Liberal, Kansas, maintained its claim to fame as the place near which, in the famous classic film "The Wizard of Oz," Dorothy was clunked on the bean with an airborne house during a tornado. Again, I should have been astute enough to smell a rat when our search for pheasants began there. Any place where witches, talking scarecrows, and munchkins are given the same status as moms, the flag, and apple pie should be viewed with suspicion. Perhaps if my hosts had made a coward of me in front of a scornful face spread across a huge screen flanked with roaring bursts of flame in order to ask a bogus Mr. Wizard where the roosters were, I would have caught on. If Toto had been paraded out as our top gun dog, that also may have been enough of a clue for me to realize that the jig was up.

People who live in places where the curvature of the earth can be readily observed in any direction, and where the tops of people's heads can be seen two hundred miles away with a good spotting scope, often get their amusement in strange ways. Kansas bird hunters are, however, most hospitable and always spend the off season looking for sports, such as people like myself, to invite for some bird hunting.

In any event, the big day finally arrived, and we traveled to the fabled land in search of cackling roosters—the wizards of KansOz. Failing to find any yellow brick roads, we traveled to the fields and croplands in a traditional way on ordinary blacktop and dust-covered country lanes.

Whenever a rooster did get up in front of me and I was able to suppress my adrenaline-pumping surprise long enough to remember to flick the safety off my shotgun and actually get a shot off, I was always given credit for crumpling the bird. Even if two or three other gunners discharged their weapons at the rocketing bird, I was congratulated with statements like, "You hit him hard on your first shot, but he went a little ways before he died. My shot missed just as he folded" and "Heck of a shot, Taylor! That bird flew toward me for a hundred yards before you killed it. What kind of choke you usin'?" I did not dwell on the puzzling phenomenon of my new-found marksmanship, since my ego and esteem increased with each heavy rooster kindly stuffed into the growing game pouch on the back of my shooting vest.

In no time, I nearly had my limit while the others were practically birdless. My virtuous companions seemed to disown any jealousy of my hunting prowess. "What a great bunch of guys!," I said to myself whenever I was reminded of my good fortune by the constant, exhausting pull on my shoulders from my impressive game bag.

Later, we tried our hand at shooting quail. I soon discovered that there were two species in our hunting area. The first appeared to be little brown-colored rascals that always scared the socks off of me by bursting from underfoot and racing off like blurry bats out of hell. The second species was soft gray and never failed to rattle my resolve while bursting from cover and zipping away at velocities approaching the speed of light. To my delight, I learned flushing quail was like stepping on a feathered land mine loaded with fast-flapping shrapnel. I even killed a couple. All by myself. However, I never told my audience that the birds which fell were not always the ones at which I aimed. Somehow, I was given the impression that they had already noticed that.

I must admit that, at one point of the hunt, I wondered if I was being led on and made the butt of a practical joke. The situation came about by my noticing several companions instantly and savagely attacking any pile of brush we encountered. It seemed like a peculiar thing to do. I asked several quail-shooting veterans about this behavior and was told that quail often use brush piles as resting places, and must be quickly attacked. Wary quail, it seemed, would run away minutes before any slow-footed quail slayer ambled to within long rifle range. The explanation sounded reasonable to me, though I kept a close watch on the expressions of the veterans as they spoke, looking for any winking, hidden mirth, or tell-tale bitten tongues.

Even during my first dash toward a brush pile, I kept an ear cocked toward my watching hunting partners for any burst of laughter, but none came. I allowed that either they were legitimate or they posed with poker faces modeled after Mt. Rushmore. As I raced with panting and rapid breath, caused not by excitement, to a low pile of brush, the air was suddenly and miraculously filled with flying quail. In the blink of a runner's eye, the sky changed from blue to a mottled brown and soft gray.

Then a strange thing happened. Time and motion seemed to stop, and the dozens of buzzing quail seemed to freeze and hang in mid-air. It was as if I were in a silent shooting gallery with no need to hurry shots at stationary targets. I carefully picked out a single quail, saw it fold with my shot, then deliberately picked a second bird, which also tumbled from the sky. Instantly, time, motion, and sound returned and the remaining quail disappeared in a blink. It was then my turn to give the Mt. Rushmore impersonation and pretend that anything less than a double on quail was far beneath me. I do not think anyone was fooled or impressed.

Being a good sport, I freely humored myself and played along with the gag my hosts pulled on me with the prairie-chicken routine. This charade seemed to be the most popular with the citizens of KansOz. They had their lines down well while seriously telling me about the elusiveness and uncanny cleverness of this mythological bird. To kill one was a great and triumphant feat. It was implied that to those lucky few who downed a prairie chicken, the door to well-earned social and political powers would be opened and that maidens would throw themselves at their hunting boots. This last tidbit of information was intriguing since I never had anyone throw themselves at my hunting boots except myself when I frequently stumbled, and I vowed that if I ever got a shot at a prairie chicken, I would shoot with deadly intent.

So as to not spoil the fun, I upheld my part of the hoax as we spent hours looking for the phantom of the bird world. It was akin to looking for leprechauns and munchkins, but what the heck, I thought, isn't hunting for fun and games? Somehow, my hosts sensed I was skeptical about the existence of this species of fowl.

Later in town, they went so far as to show me a mounted prairie chicken, posed in a strutting stance in which, I was told, the males impressed potential mates by running in place until exhausted. The mounted bird was an excellent imitation, and I erred when I speculated that some taxidermist must have worked days to produce it. Aghast, my flatland friends insisted it was the real McCoy. I quickly picked up my fumble by assuming the Mt. Rushmore look of seriousness and asked for their repentance.

Needless to say, I never was given a chance to bag a prairie chicken and watch the rush of maidens stampede in my direction, but then, there are no guarantees in hunting. Maybe someday I will again shoot roosters of KansOz, attempt wind sprints at brush piles, or pretend to look for prairie chickens just for the fun of it. All I have to do to get there is close my eyes and click the heels of my ruby boots together three times.

Chapter Fifteen
North to Adventure

 We were off on another adventure. Destination: Unclear. Time schedule: Who cared? Funds: Very limited. Enthusiasm: Endless. One spring day, Meredith and I packed our gear in the truck, waved goodbye to the known, and said hello to the unexplored as we headed north. Our trails during the next fifteen months were covered by truck, riverboat, canoe, horse, small airplane, ship, and foot as we surveyed and learned the ways of northern British Columbia, the Yukon Territory, and the coastal panhandle of Alaska.

There was no limit to the interesting places we encountered. On Montana's western plains, we camped near a bird refuge covered with migrating waterfowl and shore birds of every description. The birds were en route to their northern nesting grounds and filled the air from dawn until dusk with honks, quacks, chirps, cries, and squawks, vocalizing their impatience at spring's slow thaw of the northern marshes.

As we left the area, we were delayed by military police while a strategic missile was transported to a nearby silo. The projectile was mammoth and somehow reminded me of a horizontal version of the towering redwood trees I had seen in northern California. Unlike the ducks, geese, and other birds, I hoped the migratory programming of the huge missile remained dormant. Near the Great Falls of the Missouri River, it was enlightening to study the journals of Lewis and Clark, written in 1805 and 1806, and to compare the land we saw to the land those great explorers described. Much had changed and, from a hunter's point of view, the present did not stack up to the distant past of innumerable buffalo, sheep, grizzly bears, elk, deer, and antelope Lewis and Clark described.

Perhaps it's because I was born at the foot of the Colorado Front Range, where rolling prairies border the timbered slopes of mountains, and was raised in the shadow of 14,110-foot Pike's Peak that I have always been partial to country where the high plains meet the Rocky Mountains. It's only natural that the land along the eastern flank of Glacier National Park and the western portion of the Blackfeet Indian Reservation was much to my liking. Meredith and I spent several days visiting the reservation and park borderlands, and still saw but a glimpse of the wealth of scenery, wildlife, culture, and history of that beautiful land where the plains and mountains join.

The customs officials were very strict and straightforward. They quickly checked our vehicle and verified that it contained no contraband, refugees, terrorists, nuclear devices, or disease-bearing animals before we motored on our way.

I'm not sure how a band of bighorn rams in Banff National Park became so vain, but they certainly knew how to put on a show for tourists. The mature rams posed and strutted in front of our cameras and appeared jealous if the lenses were not directed at them. I laughed at one ram that planted his feet like a champion show dog, stretched his neck, and proudly turned his splendid horns from side to side. He seemed quite pleased to hear the photographers' clicking shutters.

The self-centered rams were much different from the shaggy mountain goats I observed at a mineral lick in Jasper National Park. These easy-going, philosophical animals viewed the world with dignified indifference. Later, we watched other mountain goats in the Yukon Territory and southeastern Alaska. After seeing these sure-footed mountaineers move across rock faces as easily as a fly traverses a wall, I concluded that no story about the goats' ability to cling to cliffs had ever been exaggerated. They strolled effortlessly over the top of the world. I envisioned the exciting adventure of hunting the underestimated mountain goat and placed the species near the top of the list of big-game animals I would like to pursue.

Meredith and I stopped in Dawson Creek, British Columbia, to snap the token photos of each other standing beside the famous Milepost Zero of the Alaskan Highway, the official start of one of the most historic, scenic, and talked-about roads ever built. This was to be my second, Meredith's first, journey along the interesting road that weaves through the heart of the Land of the Midnight Sun.

It's odd how the highlights of travels often happen not from carefully planned agendas, but from stumbling into unknown opportunities. Such was the case on our trek. Moments before we departed for the North Country, I ran into a friend on the main street of our small town. While chatting about our proposed journey, my friend mentioned he had relatives—an aunt, uncle, and cousins—who owned one of the lodges along the Alaskan Highway, and suggested that we stop to visit them. This scrap of information proved to be a key that unlocked many adventures during the coming summer and fall.

Leaving Dawson Creek behind, we drove north into the northwestern frontier of Canada and the vast, pristine wilderness beyond. The closer we got to my friend's relatives' lodge, the more excited I became. We had left the rolling forestlands and had entered country lined with steep-sloped mountains and fast-moving creeks. I sensed that the area we had entered was a sportsman's dream, a wildlife paradise. The next few months proved those first impressions correct.

We turned off the washboard, dust-choked highway into the parking lot of the lodge. The buildings had been resurrected from an abandoned military post and converted into living quarters, a cafe, motel, and garage. Four rangy-looking horses dozed near a large weathered barn. I noticed a nearby hay meadow, the first sign of agriculture in several hundred miles, wrenched from the grasp of the persistent willows and poplar trees that thrive in the abundant annual rainfall. At that moment, a small airplane buzzed the top of a nearby hill, made a low pass over the grassy, level shoulder of the highway that served as a landing strip, and then made a 180-degree turn past the far end of the strip. The pilot, seeing that the runway was clear of livestock, children, dogs, moose, vehicles and such, landed the plane and bounced to a stop beside several barrels of aviation fuel under a faded wind-sock. I realized then that the lodge also included an airport.

The lodge complex, like many along the highway, was nearly a self-contained town. Weekly supplies were handed down from the trailer of an eighteen-wheel rig, and a semi-reliable telephone connected these isolated posts to the rest of the world.

Everything else was up to the people who lived in the remote North. Many children were educated at home through correspondence courses. Each lodge provided water, waste systems, and electricity from diesel-powered generators to the many outbuildings surrounding the central complex. During winter's fifty-below-zero temperatures, many owners attend the precious generators as if the machines were ailing children; a mechanical failure at those critical times could spell disaster.

With the nearest town sometimes hundreds of miles away, it was no wonder these lodges served as the hubs of their surrounding communities. The locals, trappers, miners, Indians, outfitters, highway-maintenance workers, young homesteaders, and old pioneers gathered around tables covered with coffee cups or beer bottles, depending on the time of day, and visited while watching the vehicles travel up and down the highway.

We hit it off well with my friend's kin. They were friendly, hard-working, and hard-playing people who treated us like part of the family. There was always much work to be done at their lodge. During the lengthy summer days when the tourist season was at its peak, the cafe, motel, camp-ground, and garage required many eighteen-hour work days. This was in addition to building, maintenance, tending a small herd of cattle, putting up hay for winter feed, and numerous other outside projects that could be done only during the warm months. Meredith and I pitched in to help and, by doing so, we saw and learned much of the North Country. Our rewards were the sights, friendships, and experiences lost to the average traveler. I remember how fascinated I was to watch the locals fish. We had set aside a day for relaxing, not because the never-ending work was done, but because all work and no play is a foolish way to spend a life anywhere. I became curious the night before we went fishing when a three-pound package of frozen moose meat was taken from the freezer to thaw.

The following morning found us nosing our way up a twenty-yard-wide stream in a homemade river boat. The plywood craft had a square bow, a flat bottom, and was nearly eighteen feet long. The powerful motor was equipped with a jet foot instead of a propeller. The boat was designed to travel in shallow water, providing passage for mechanized man through country where no road had been pushed or airstrip cleared. We came to a huge, willow-covered bottom, miles long, and landed the boat on a sandy shore. The stream meandered in lazy turns, the bottoms of deep pools clouded by the silty glacial run-off from the mountains upstream. I was told Stone sheep were often seen among the standing skeletons of fire-killed tree on the opposite mountainside. Embedded in the wet sand near the boat were aging wolf tracks and the distinct, fresh tracks of a single caribou.

We had just started to assemble our fishing rods when an Indian woman emerged from the forest across the stream. She was clad in beaded moosehide boots, blue jeans, a beautiful handmade leather vest over a wool shirt, and wore a fluorescent pink scarf around her head. At her side on a leash was the most ferocious-looking dog I had ever seen. Our fishing hosts recognized the smiling woman, exchanged greetings, and offered to ferry her and her savage companion to our side of the river. She declined the offer with a shake of her head and spoke a few happy, inaudible words while pointing upstream.

I watched the woman walk to two logs held together by a wooden deck, tie the dog to the raft, and pole across the calm, deep pool. The dog, accustomed to the routine, swam easily beside the crude raft. Before joining us, the woman walked to a clump of tall willows, found a heavy fishing line tied to one of the limbs and, hand over hand, reeled the set line from the bottom of the pool. A look of disappointment showed on her face as a large, bare hook surfaced at the end of the line. She immediately reached into her shirt pocket and found a piece of meat. She threaded the new bait onto the hook and cast it into the depths of the pool.

The woman approached our group with polite, cheerful answers to our hosts' pleasantries and, with shy glances, acknowledged Meredith and I as strangers. A moment later, she continued downstream on a faint path that led to the Alaskan Highway, many miles away.

The woman lived in a small village a few miles above the area we fished and was on her way to do some errands in town. She expected to be gone several days. The mean-looking dog that escorted her was for protection against grizzly bears. This woman of the wilderness matter-of-factly explained that she was afraid to travel the river path at night without the dog. I marveled at the difference between this light-hearted lady and her southern, citified sisters as she set out on her shopping trip. Soon thoughts of the Indian woman were pushed aside as our optimistic group strung out along the sandy shore. Meredith tried casting a small fly into an eddy behind a rock in midstream and landed a grayling. Pitching my standard offering of a small spinner across the stream, I hooked a pound-sized Dolly Varden trout that flashed in the clear, sunlit water.

One of our hosts, Bob, used different tactics, which I watched with great interest. He slowly strolled beside a deep pool and seemed as interested in finding a comfortable seat as in selecting a suitable fishing spot. In addition to his fishing rod, he carried a tackle box and the package of moose meat. I was amazed to see him carve off a chunk of meat big enough to feed a grown housecat, stab it onto a large hook, and lob the bait into the deep pool with a splash that sounded like a brick hitting the water. The bottom-fishing angler then sat back and smoked a cigarette while watching the huge cumulus clouds in the deep blue sky.

Soon I saw his fishing rod begin to dip occasionally as a fish tugged at the lump of meat. Bob calmly watched his rod but made no move toward it for several minutes. Only when the tugs became frantic and constant did he move to reel in a five-pound Dolly Varden. I pondered the saying, "When in Rome, do as the Romans." I was not exactly in Caesar's back yard but, in a few short moments, I found myself lobbing a good-sized piece of moose meat into the deep pools.

It was interesting how the long summer days affected people. We were far enough north that, during June, the sky never darkened at night. The twilight of dusk only merged with the dawn of a new day. This increased summer daylight was matched only by the corresponding increase in human energy and activity. Spurred by what seemed to be a combination of a desire to pack as much into each day as possible before the cold, dark winter arrived, and a change in biological metabolism triggered by the abundance of light, people of all ages appeared to be in constant motion. Rising early in the morning, the Northern folks buzzed around all day and most of the sunlit night, paused for a few hours of sleep during the wee hours of morning, then jumped up to do it all over again.

The perfect example of this phenomenon occurred at the lodge on July 1, Dominion Day—Canada's anniversary of confederation of the provinces.

Never missing an opportunity for a celebration, our hosts invited the entire community to a traditional barbecue centered around the sizzling steaks of a fat steer. It was a gala affair filled with much laughter and socializing. A baseball game was organized between spurts of drizzling rain. Men and women, young and old, gathered at the rustic ball diamond for a rousing, though somewhat damp, game.

After fielding a soggy grounder in right field, I glanced at my watch and stared in disbelief at the hands showing 3 a.m.

Black bears, grizzlies, and wolves were common in the area around the lodge. Many times we saw non-aggressive, free-loading black bears among the buildings. A cream-colored husky-cross dog, a pet allowed to roam free, took seriously his duty of driving black bears away and would immediately attack any that he saw. If, however, a grizzly bear came around, he refused to leave his owner's side. Wolves routinely traveled through the area, usually as quietly as a wisp of wind but occasionally announcing their whereabouts with beautiful, eerie howls in the night.

It was generally agreed that these predators killed cattle and horses now and then, but not enough to warrant eradication of the wolves and bears. Any loss of livestock was offset by revenues gained from winter wolf pelts. In addition, grizzlies and black bears put many sportsmen's dollars into outfitters' and guides' bank accounts. Few people of the North advocated total extermination of the large carnivores; likewise, though, total protection from hunting was considered an unwise idea. Because wolves and bears were hunted, they tended to keep their distance from man and his domain. The classification of the grizzly as a game animal and the wolf as a furbearer resulted in a balance between nature and man, where all could co-exist in perpetuity.

During our stay at the lodge, we met many British Colombian and Yukon big-game outfitters and guides as they traveled the highway. It was interesting to talk to several individuals whose names I had read in hunting magazines and books. In conversation, names of famous big-game regions, the holy lands of hunters, came to life, including the Bonnet Plume and Pelly Rivers, Ruby Range, Atlin Lake, Dease Lake, Watson Lake, the Cassiar, Muskwa and Prophet Rivers.

One of the outfitters invited Meredith and me to inspect his hunting area with him as he made final preparations at his base camps for the approaching hunting seasons. Soon, we were looking down on endless miles of game-filled mountains through the windows of the outfitter's Super Cub.

The airplane buzzed up the valley, walled by steep mountains topped with occasional snow fields, descended into a willow-filled clearing, and finally bounced to a stop on a short landing strip that had been cleared by hand

Tory Taylor glasses for dall sheep in the vast mountains of the Yukon Territory.

and horsepower. Nearby was one of the outfitter's base camps. Numerous tents would be set up and horses trailed to camp before hunting season began. We carried some supplies to a cache in a windowless log cabin before we lifted off again.

Back in the air, we skimmed over beautiful saber-toothed peaks while looking for mountain goats and Stone sheep. As we approached another base camp, the outfitter circled the area searching for a dozen of his horses. These horses stayed year-round at the base camp foraging for themselves much as the wildlife did for the winter. We finally spotted the multi-colored dots of the horse herd, then landed beside a classic log cabin, complete with moose antlers hanging above the porch. The cabin was used as a kitchen and hunting lodge for the camp.

While unloading supplies here, the outfitter told us some interesting stories about the horses we'd seen. One big brown gelding, named "Sixty Below," had been kept near the outfitter's home ranch as a colt. The band of horses he ran with was periodically checked by an Indian during the winter. In January, a terrible cold snap hit the North Country. The Indian found the young gelding nearly frozen, his brain and body numbed by the penetrating cold. The Indian led the frosted animal back to the ranch, put him in the shelter of a warm barn and saved the horse's life. When the Indian finished with the colt, he looked at the thermometer; the mercury registered at sixty degrees below zero.

Another of the outfitter's horse stories was about Marcia, an ancient, gray-muzzled mare that once gave a guide the ride of his life. The mare had spent years in the bush and was used to fending off inquisitive visits by wolves and grizzlies. A jolly Indian guide with a great respect for grizzlies once used the mare to lead a hunter in search of moose. Rounding a clump of willows, the guide and Marcia surprised a sow grizzly with two cubs. Instantly, the cubs fled and the sow charged from less than a hundred yards away. The guide had no time to react before the gutsy mare laid back her ears, squealed angrily and counter-attacked the grizzly. The helpless, wide-eyed rider could do nothing but hold onto the saddle horn with both hands and, from an unchosen front-row seat, watch the two animals race toward each other. Just before they would have collided, the bear spun around and followed her cubs, and the shaken guide was trotted back and forth on the fearless, snorting Marcia.

A few weeks later, I was back at the base-camp cabin and saw for myself this fighting streak in Marcia. A caribou had been shot, and I tagged along to help pack it back to camp. Marcia was among the horses we used, and she stood dozing as we skinned and quartered the caribou. The hunter wanted the antlers sawed from the skull and the beautiful hide left whole for a rug. After completing the job, we rolled the hide into a bundle and tied it with a cord. When Marcia saw the roll of animal hair on the ground, she had a fit. In a flash, the mare was pounding the innocuous hide with her front hooves. Even when held in my arms, she snarled and bit at the fuzzy bundle. Only after we tied the caribou hide onto a packhorse did Marcia calm down.

Several times during the summer and fall, Meredith and I traveled with the outfitter and explored on horse, foot and airplane the silent backcountry of northern British Columbia.

What a big-game country we found! We saw moose, caribou, and Stone sheep nearly everywhere we went. Mountain goats were common up high; grizzly and wolf tracks could be seen along stream beds; black bear, wolverine, elk, and mule deer were also present. How I wished I could ramble around that country with my rifle. Someday, I told myself, someday.

One of our journeys put us in the heart of Stone-sheep range. As near as I could determine, we were within a very short distance of the spot where, in 1936, Mr. L.S. Chadwick shot an enormous ram with horns more than fifty inches long. Although the country was probably much the same, the hunting scene had changed since the famous Chadwick ram grazed these northern Rocky Mountains. Many outfitted and guided hunters now combed those same mountains each year and killed some nice rams, but gone are the days of hunting for record-book rams in virgin country.

The summer sped by and we realized the winter would soon be upon us. Meredith and I said goodbye to the wonderful friends we had made and the wild country we had seen. Both of us agreed our absence would be temporary. We vowed to return for another visit to that beautiful country and continue to explore its waterways, silent forests, and towering mountains. One of our next stops was at the historic town of Whitehorse, Yukon Territory. There, the decaying riverboats, memorials to the booming gold-rush days, sat next to the mighty Yukon River. A fascinating cross-section of people mixed on the streets, reflecting the many facets and lifestyles of the North. Gold miners, doctors, trappers, lawyers, bush pilots, Indians, mounties, and homesteaders all rubbed elbows in the center. We explored several roads that branched out from Whitehorse and led to scenic lakes, small villages, ghost towns, and other attractions.

West of Whitehorse, we visited the famous Kluane Game Sanctuary. It was there that we climbed the lower peaks of the St. Elias Range and watched Dall sheep graze across the talus slopes. Several bushes held clumps of shed hair, snagged in the limbs by rubbing animals. The soft, downy undercoat seemed longer than that of other wild sheep. Large lakes in the area provided us with excellent canoeing. We toured along their shores, stopping to explore on foot and to camp wherever and whenever the spirit moved us.

We stayed in the Kluane Lake area for a few days and visited historic Burwash Landing. It was there that the pioneer outfitters, Gene and Louie Jacquot, had their home and base of operation. We also learned that Burwash Landing has the questionable fame of having recorded the incredible temperature of eighty degrees below zero.

During one of our side trips, we discovered a fairly well-made shack on the shore of a forty-mile-long lake. The ten-foot-by-twenty-foot, flat-roofed, one-room building was surrounded by high, rolling mountains. At the far end of the lake, another range of jagged mountains pointed to the sky and beckoned to our wandering spirits. A reconnaissance of the country surrounding the cabin revealed the presence of grizzly bear, mountain sheep, moose, wolves, ptarmigan, and other wildlife. During the calm of early morning, rings made by feeding fish could be seen on the glassy surface of the lake. Meredith and I agreed the shack looked like a perfect place to pass a northern winter. Through inquiries and investigation, we contacted the owner of the rustic abode, who gave us permission to use the shack as our winter home. Another adventure began to unfold.

The shack was near the end of a road that was passable only during the mild summer months. After branching off the Alaskan Highway, the road snaked its way through twenty miles of dense forest, becoming more difficult to travel with each mile. We realized that once the first snow closed the road to travel, trips to civilization for supplies would be out of the question.

We carefully made a shopping list for quantities of food to last us at least four months. A final late-fall trip to Whitehorse provided us with the necessary supplies for winter. The last two miles back to the shack were traveled by canoe. We piled box upon box in the canoe and launched the laden craft into the rolling waves. The canoe sat alarmingly low in the water, and paddling the weighted vessel was like maneuvering a water-soaked log. It was a satisfying feeling to have stacks of food and firewood at the shack when winter sent the temperatures plummeting. The lake froze during the first week of December and, after several days of cold weather, a thin layer of ice appeared on the quiet bays and along the shoreline. By the next day, the entire lake was covered by a couple of inches of ice. At the end of a few more days of bitter cold, we were able to walk on the foot of clear, black ice that locked the lake. Winter had arrived. Visions of ice-fishing vanished as the ice continued to thicken to a depth of more than five feet. But the deep ice paved the way for sight-seeing excursions over the length of the lake and served as a highway for man and beast. Our tracks mingled with those of otters, coyotes, wolverines, and wolves.

Across the lake, the dense timber rose several thousand feet before giving way to a series of round mountains. The slopes of the range were the breeding ground and winter range for several hundred Dall sheep. Meredith and I spent hours at the spotting scope, watching the white sheep. Occasionally, old rams with heavy, full-curled, amber horns appeared in the herds during the breeding season and then vanished to places known only to the sheep.

From the frozen shore in front of our winter home one overcast day, I scanned the peaks for game. Suddenly, I saw an animal with a gray body and white head, neck, and legs. My first thought was caribou, but I then remembered the locals telling me no caribou lived in the area. I increased the power of the spotting scope, saw the curling horns of the strange animal, and realized I was looking at a Fannin ram. An instant later, I noticed movement near the ram and focused on a dozen snow-white Dall companions of the gray sheep. Whereas the Dall sheep were nearly invisible in the dim light and snow-covered landscape, the Fannin ram stood out plainly against the white background. The handsome ram's silver coat covered his back and sides and clearly outlined his white rump. He was unquestionably one of the most beautiful wild sheep I have ever seen.

We kept a temperature record throughout the winter. It was fun to see the average temperature grow colder and colder with each passing week, until late January, when a warm wind skyrocketed the temperatures back into the twenty-above-zero range. The coldest temperature we recorded was fifty degrees below zero.

We had been curious to see how long the sun would remain in view during the Winter Solstice, the shortest day of the year. This official declaration of the first day of winter was thirty days too late—winter had already arrived.

Nevertheless, we hiked through powdery snow to the top of a nearby peak to document the sun at high noon that day. The distant, blazing orb barely cleared the jagged white peaks on the southern horizon before descending. The great, fiery giver of life cast a half-light on the white landscape and radiated no warmth on the frozen north.

A Chinook wind blew for several days during the first week of February. The temperatures, which had been below freezing for months, suddenly rose to about fifty degrees. The powdery snow settled, bare ground appeared here and there, and puddles formed on the lake's thick ice. The huge flocks of snow-white ptarmigan cackled their approval and became more active as they searched for seeds among the willows above timberline.

The snow on the road leading to the Alaskan Highway settled enough for travel during the Chinook wind. We reconnected the battery that had been stored in the shack to prevent it from freezing, started the truck, and motored into Whitehorse in time for the annual Rendezvous. What a colorful celebration the Rendezvous was. No case of cabin fever remained uncured after days of dogsled racing, packing and wood-sawing competitions, plus feasting, dancing, and plenty of laughing.

A grueling event—and one popular with spectators—was the flour-sack backpacking contest. The person who carried the most hundred-pound sacks won. This event was to commemorate the gold rush of 1898 and the hardy prospectors who walked to the northern gold fields. Many of the contestants staggered under loads approaching half a ton. With all the activity and pent-up merriment, it was easy to understand why people came from as far away as Alaska, British Columbia, and the Northwest territories to participate.

A few weeks later, at the lakeside cabin, we packed a picnic, hopped into the truck, and drove out on the ice to the far end of the lake. There, a pack of wolves lay snoozing in the sun on the shore ice after feeding on a moose. As we approached them, they trotted off in separate directions and faded into the protection of the surrounding forest. We stopped the vehicle, spread the picnic on the hood, and listened to the wolves howl back and forth. With the sun gleaming off the jagged, white peaks around us, the melodies of the wolves regrouping floated across the silent land. We enjoyed a unique lunch in the wonderful northern wilderness.

The promise of spring was in the air, and we were restless to travel again. Our belongings were gathered and loaded in the truck. Before leaving, we stood on the shore in front of the shack and recalled the winter we had spent isolated on the long lake. We thought about the mystery of dancing northern lights and the dark blue-velvet sky of the frigid winter twilight. We said our farewells to the sheep, moose, wolves, and ptarmigan.

Our next stop was at the Chilkat River drainage in the southeast panhandle of Alaska. Along this valley, thousands of bald eagles migrate, eating salmon and other fish from the nearby ocean. It was a marvelous sight to see as many as thirty of these great birds resting in a cottonwood tree. The breathtaking glacier-covered mountains rising from the sea were the home of a healthy population of mountain goats. On several occasions, we climbed the steep slopes to photograph the shaggy animals. Grouse drummed everywhere from the timbered hillsides.

My enthusiasm to explore the brushy riverbottoms was cooled when I saw the gigantic track of a brown bear. The huge hind tracks of the bear dwarfed my size-twelve boot tracks. I would have been thrilled to see the bear that made those tracks—at a distance. We spent several weeks exploring the fiords by canoe and on foot before embarking on the Alaskan ferry and touring the Inside Passage on our return to the lower forty eight states.

An uneasy feeling had been bothering me for a few months. I didn't know what caused me to be troubled until we returned to the sweeping, open spaces of the high plains meeting the mountains in northern Montana. There, I realized I had unknowingly been homesick for the sight of rolling grasslands carved by cottonwood-lined streams flowing from the distant mountains. Meredith gave me a questioning look as I happily began singing the old, familiar tune: "Oh, give me a home, where the buffalo roam, where the deer and the antelope play..."

Our fifteen-month odyssey came to an end.

Chapter Sixteen
White Wanderers in the Colorado Rockies

 We three oldest Taylor brothers missed the boat when we were growing up in Colorado. Yes, it is true that when we lived there we hunted elk and, sure, we killed our share of buck deer. It is also correct that we ended numerous careers of antelope, but before we left the state in order to lead lives elsewhere, we all made big mistakes by not hunting mountain goats in the jagged, spectacular peaks of the Colorado Rockies.

Thank goodness little brother Cec did not follow the example we elder siblings set. Instead, he religiously applied for a goat tag until he was among the chosen ones. For several years, Cec had been obsessed with the notion of hunting mountain goats. Each year before he applied, I assured him that if he drew a tag, I would help him hunt for the shaggy, white animals. When the time came, Cec and I met—three days before the season opened—in the rejuvenated ghost town Hardgrove cabin, cradled deep in the heart of 14,000-foot peaks. Now one more story, a once in a lifetime story, was about to unfold for Cec.

This was not to be a four-wheel-drive hunt, nor was it to even be horse-supported. Instead, we would do it the way mountain-goat hunting was intended to be done. Early one morning, with the sun's first rays melting the frost on yellow aspen leaves, we shouldered heavy packs containing all that we would need for several days and started for the highcountry.

By late afternoon, we reached timberline near the hunting area and found a place to camp. Anyone who has ever hunted in mountain-goat country knows that the chance of finding a level place to sleep is about the same as seeing one hundred dollar bills flutter from the sky. Cec chose a relatively flat spot along the side of a large fallen tree, and I picked a comfortable deer bed under the protective limbs of a spruce tree. The often-used deer bed actually wasn't a bad sleeping place—as long as I slept in the position of a bedded deer.

Until dark, we glassed and glassed the surrounding mountains, though we spent as much time looking at the autumn beauty around us as we did looking for animals.

The next day was our last scouting day before the hunting season opened. We used the time as best as we could. By mid-afternoon, we had spotted ten bighorn rams, three large buck mule deer, numerous elk, and perhaps fifty to sixty mountain goats. The elk-breeding season was in full swing. During our first night camping, bulls periodically disturbed the silence with their urgent bugling. Early one morning, I watched through my spotting scope as a medium-sized bull strolled slowly through an opening. When a second bull appeared, I called to Cec, "There are two bulls over on that hill. No, three. Now four! Wow! Five. Six. Here comes number seven!" The group of seven bulls, all as similar as peas in a pod, ambled through the opening. I believed they had been driven away from the herds by larger bulls and together were checking out the neighborhood.

Of the goats we had watched, a group of five large adults, which appeared to all be billies, interested us most. During our days of scouting, the goats showed themselves to us each morning and evening. Whereas all of the other goats we watched moved very little, these five acted like spooked deer. Just at first light, the group left the alpine slopes where it fed all night, scampered quickly into thick timber, descended several thousand feet down the mountain, and spent the day near a steep, unapproachable rock outcropping surrounded by tall trees. Just before dark, the five goats climbed back up the mountain to their feeding grounds far above treeline. It was strange behavior, but more important, it was predictable behavior.

On the afternoon before season opened, we goat hunting, eye-strained, and sore-shouldered brothers figured out a strategy and plan of attack. The plan called for us to move our camp to an area well below the place where the five billy goats fed, spend a very quiet night, ambush the five at daylight on their way to their daytime hiding place and, finally, backpack a dead goat off of the mountain before dark. Simple. Piece of cake. Nothing to it.

As we moved camp to a new location, we walked past a large, wind-tortured tree growing in the center of what appeared to be the crossroads of the five goats' travels. Each time we watched them, they had walked near this particular area. Cec stopped to study the area and the tree before he said to me, "I want to be right here at daylight tomorrow." I agreed that it seemed like the spot to be.

At the new camp, our luck to find a level place to sleep again failed, though the site had several other merits. It was in a grove of twisted and dwarfed aspens that commanded a spectacular view of the high peaks around us and of the thin, silver ribbon of stream far below. A herd of elk had very recently visited the aspen grove. Their rank, musky smell was nearly overpowering. I shook out my sleeping bag onto the middle of the grove and joked to Cec: "Maybe the goats will smell us and think we are elk."

"Right," Cec said flatly. "Then if we can add some goat smell to the way we already stink, people are really going to be glad to see us when we get home."

After our aspen-grove camp was organized, we searched for the five billies. We had put all of our eggs in one basket and counted on the goats to continue their unusual routine. As the afternoon wore on, both Cec and I kept our fingers crossed and hoped we had done the right thing. Suddenly, I spotted a goat standing on a talus slope in the timber a thousand yards away. Cec and I soon located all five goats as they climbed the mountainside, heading for their feeding area. Our hopes soared.

As the five billies climbed the slope, we were able to look at them closely through the spotting scope. They were absolutely beautiful, five mature billies in new winter coats, regal animals in the prime of their lives. They were the undisputed masters of the cliffs and seemed not ashamed to display their pride. As I watched the powerful animals climb, I again reinforced my belief that the mountain goat was unquestionably the most underrated trophy big-game animal in North America. There were deer organizations by the score, numerous elk clubs, several big-horn sheep groups, but few hunters wanted to sing the praises of these worthy, fascinating animals that live in the clouds. Perhaps someday, I thought, the mountain goat will be elevated to the high status it deserves.

That evening, just before dark, we walked a short distance from our camp to a place where we could view the feeding area of the five billies. We found the goats exactly where we thought we would and watched them from a distance until the mountainside faded into darkness.

That night, I slept like a baby, perched on the side of a mountain; camped with my brother in rugged peaks. Five adult billies, the object of our mission, grazed within a mile of camp; what possible worries could have kept me from sleep? Cec, on the other hand, didn't fair so well. With the desire to kill a goat driving him, the pressure of possessing a tag, and the responsibility of carrying the rifle that puts more weight on the mind than it does on the shoulder, his thoughts tumbled questions in his head all night. Would the five billies still be on the mountain in the morning? Would he be able to climb to other goats if they were gone? Would he get a clean shot?

The night passed, and the eastern sky began to glow softly, bringing the first morning of mountain-goat season with the new day. Cec and I had a light breakfast, not much more than hot drinks heated over the small gas stove. We each made a last-minute check of our hunting packs as shooting light advanced.

Soon, we looked at each other with excitement gleaming in our eyes and, with silent nods, announced we were ready.

We advanced slowly up a ridge above camp. Our excitement increased with each step as we neared the feeding area of the billies. As we approached the wind-tormented tree that seemed to be the hub of the goats' travels, our moods became even more intense. Cec slowly walked to the right side of the tree while I eased to its left. As we stepped from behind the tree's wide limbs, we simultaneously spotted a feeding mountain goat less than two hundred yards above.

Quickly and carefully, we retreated behind the trunk of the tree. Cec steadied his .270's stock on the tree while I knelt behind and whispered encouragement. As we watched, a second billy, with slightly larger horns, appeared. Cec pointed the rifle's barrel in the goat's direction. He was cool as a cucumber, biding his time in a perfect hunting situation.

Then the billy turned exactly broadside and stood completely still. The .270 sent a 130-grain bullet on its way, and the billy died instantly on his feet. Three other billies came quickly shuffling into view from behind a knoll, looked us and the situation over, then rapidly continued their stiff-legged gait to parts unknown.

By late afternoon, the Brothers Two had packed the boned meat plus the full hide and head of the goat from the mountain. We again enjoyed the security and comfort of the ghost-town cabin, and the previous Taylor clan mistake of not climbing to the top of the world in search of mountain goats was partially rectified. It certainly was high time to do so.

Chapter Seventeen
Henry's Hunt

 May 22. I received a bighorn sheep permit. The Goddess Chip of the Wyoming Game and Fish Department's computer smiled on me. Just drawing a sheep license was thrilling, and suddenly my entire world revolved around it. Nothing was the same as I reappraised everything I owned that involved hunting; everything had to be perfect. No piece of equipment, gear, or horse tack was left unchecked. Most important, my rifle and ammunition were tried time and time again. The bullet groups were more than adequate but rarely satisfied my unusually fussy standards.

July 18 - August 5. Meredith and I trucked the horses to nearby mountains and explored new country. We saw wildlife aplenty, amazing mountains, chunks of petrified wood too heavy to lift, and witnessed an exceptionally violent thunderstorm that flooded our camp. Meredith found the complete bleached skull and antlers of a big bull elk, apparently a winter kill. The antlers had six long, heavy points on one side and seven on the other. We cached the antlers in the limbs of a pine tree, with hopes of retrieving them the following year. The entire trip was relaxing and wonderful.

August 9 - 22. We prepared for an autumn of hunting. Meredith was in perpetual motion from daylight until dark organizing, packing, and gathering gear. A slow-healing back injury hampered me as I struggled to reshoe the horses.

August 26 - September 9. Meredith and I spent three leisurely days packing our sheep camp into the mountains where I would guide Henry, the first sheep hunter of my outfitting career.

It was not yet full light when we climbed onto our horses. We needed an early start on the twenty-five mile trail to base camp. The clatter of shod hooves on granite seemed unusually penetrating in the quiet twilight of the clear, calm morning. Henry was the last in line. He was a large man and rode my biggest horse, Honey, a buckskin mare. Between us was the packhorse I led, a blue roan gelding with a great sense of humor. I was on a quick, well-muscled sorrel mare and urged her up the mountain at a steady walk. Not all horses could do what I asked my horses to do that day. It would take a good horse to travel the miles and terrain we had to cover.

Meredith and I had already set up our camp at the edge of a beautiful meadow. Horse feed and level, sheltered campsites were very scarce in these mountains; we were lucky to find such an ideal spot at the edge of sheep country. It was a snug camp with a wood-burning stove in each of the tents, a sheltered place for our horse gear and saddles, plenty of wholesome food, log stools, pole washstand, a small plywood table, kitchen table, tools, and many other items for a complete hunting camp. It was to be my first camp as a licensed outfitter, and I wanted everything to be perfect.

We had a layover day in camp before sheep season opened. We fished a nearby lake until we had enough cutthroat trout to make a tasty supper. That time gave Henry and I an opportunity to visit and evaluate each other. Before we left for hunting camp, I had taken Henry to a public shooting range to check his rifle. His shooting was satisfactory and, during our conversations, I developed more and more respect for his sportsmanship and enjoyment of hunting. I knew it would be a pleasure to guide him. Henry told me about the many calls and letters he had received from outfitters after he had drawn his sheep license. He admitted it was difficult to choose an outfitter since so many of them promised him the moon if he booked with them. I told him I promised nothing except an honest effort at an enjoyable hunt.

Leaving Meredith to watch camp and care for the horses, Henry and I walked from base camp the afternoon before sheep season opened. Our plan was to backpack camp somewhere near timberline so that we could be there early the first morning of season and spend as much time as possible in sheep country. I kept a wary eye on the clouds that raced overhead. Two nights earlier, a tremendous thunderstorm had shook our camp with frequent lightning strikes and drenched the land with rain.

Henry was a keen observer of nature and marveled at the many fresh elk tracks around our timberline spike camp. He laughed in disbelief when he saw me frying inch-thick, platter-sized hamburgers over the small gas stove. I told him to enjoy the treat while he could because there were no more hamburger stands for miles and lightweight food was on the menu for the next few days. Shortly after we retired to our bedrolls, a bull elk gave a multi-noted bugle near the tent. I drifted to sleep during this beautiful lullaby.

The first day of sheep season was magnificent. We spent it searching every nook and cranny for a ram. Our pace was deliberate and slow. Twice we located bands with legal, three-quarter-curl rams, but each time the spotting scope told us we had not found the ram Henry wanted. Evening met us high on a bare ridge at our second camp, where miles of rugged sheep country laid at our feet.

The following morning, our destination was a remote valley I had briefly hunted a few years before. It was rough country, seldom visited, and what I hoped was an excellent home for tough granddaddy rams. My enthusiasm increased with each step; we were headed for sheep-hunter's heaven. We hunted the valley that afternoon and the following morning, only to find ewes and lambs and no stronghold of heavy-horned rams. We left for another prospective sheep area. Before midday, we eased to an observation point high above a valley filled with jumbled rocks and giant glaciers. Far below us, I picked up the moving white rumps with my binoculars. The spotting scope revealed five rams, the largest a magnificent sheep. His extremely large-curled, heavy horns had slightly broomed tips that came up even with the bridge of his Roman nose.

Henry looked through the scope, then turned toward me with a smile on his sunburned face. We started the stalk immediately. I had promised myself I would never go anywhere that would mean risking a fall that could injure or kill. Twice during Henry's hunt, I broke that promise. The stalk for the large ram was one of those times. Had I not trusted Henry to be double-tough and capable, I never would have attempted the stalk.

The route was not only dangerous, but seemed jinxed from the start. That jinx was caused by the old ram. Under his generalship, the five rams bedded down in an impregnable position that commanded an unobstructed view of at least seven hundred yards in all directions. The only two possible routes of approach were blocked by wind and a two-day march around and over a mountain to approach the rams from above. For the remainder of the day, Henry and I attempted to creep within rifle range, only to be frustrated with each try. We hoped the bedded rams would move in the late afternoon, but they seemed content to rest until dark. Time ran out on us.

Our backpack camp was more than a thousand vertical feet above us and several miles away at an elevation of more than 13,000 feet. The route to our spike camp was through a nightmare of rock, cliffs, and rimrock. Darkness was near when the wind changed direction and we decided to try a stalk. We were three hundred yards from the bedded rams when a steady gust of wind pushed us from the back. I groaned to myself and saw only a glimpse of the rams before they disappeared up a steep rock draw. We had tried our best and failed. We turned around and started the quiet, thoughtful climb toward camp.

The following day, we returned to base camp, rested, over indulged in Meredith's cooking, and recharged our spirits for another try at a ram. Well aware that the number of hunting days remaining was limited, Henry and I set out again for sheep country.

The seventh day was the one we had waited for. We again climbed to the high ridges and, early in the morning, I spotted a fine ram. Henry didn't hesitate when he looked through the spotting scope and announced that this was the ram he wanted.

The animal was bedded at the top of a talus slope, and a half-curl ram laid twenty yards below. Though we were nearly two miles away, we judged the terrain was favorable for a stalk and memorized the route. My greatest fear was that we might spook other sheep in the area. I cautiously glassed in all directions as we crept along. We planned to sneak to a cliff directly above the bedded rams and were out of their sight the entire stalk. More than an hour later, we paused five hundred yards from the cliff to rest and look around.

It was there that I spotted a third ram bedded several hundred yards above the large ram. It was now impossible to reach the cliff above the large ram without exposing ourselves to this third ram which faced away from us and dozed heavily in the warm sun. Henry and I agreed that our only chance was to move slowly past the sleeping third ram and reach the cliff. It was a risky move, but the only one we had. We gambled again, and this time we won, as Henry reached the cliff, peeked over the edge, and spied the large ram bedded two hundred yards below. Henry rested his rifle on a large rock and paused to release some of the tension of the stalk. Finally, he was ready and carefully placed his first shot. The ram staggered to his feet only to be anchored with a second shot.

No words were necessary as we looked at the dead ram, then at each other. Our smiles said it all. The next few hours and days passed quickly. Henry yodeled loudly as we walked into base camp that evening with the impressive sheep horns tied on his pack. Meredith guessed we had killed a ram before she emerged from the cook tent. While Henry and I told her about the final hunt, she quickly prepared a feast of sheep tenderloin and Rocky Mountain oysters. The following day, the three of us returned to the kill site and packed the remaining meat to base camp on the horses. I fleshed the ram's cape, turned the ears and lips, and salted the hide.

The next morning, we left the mountains. I lashed the ram's horns on top of the loaded packhorse with a diamond hitch. The horns were displayed in a place of honor. Henry's eyes were proudly riveted on the horns, and I could not help but tease him: "Holler if those things fall off, Henry."

"Only if I happen to notice," he retorted.

We both laughed as I started my horse down the trail.

September 10. I said good-bye to Henry at the trailhead, reshod my saddle mare in a drizzling rain, nursed a sore throat, and prepared to return to the mountains to hunt sheep for myself.

September 11. I rode to camp in a soaking snowstorm. Late that afternoon, it was a wonderful sight to see Meredith waving to me from the door of the dry, warm tent.

September 13 - 15. Snow.

September 16 - 18. The storm cleared after dumping a foot of wet snow. Meredith went by herself on a three-day hike while I recuperated from my coughing sickness.

September 19. This was the first day I hunted for my ultimate trophy. I would settle for nothing less than an old, broomed ram. Meredith accompanied me to sheep country, but we didn't see any sheep.

September 20. Snow. Two friends, Tom and Ray, stopped by our camp. Ray had a sheep license, and the two of them were searching for a ram. We decided to team up.

September 21. The four of us left camp together. Later, Ray and I climbed to sheep country while Meredith and Tom fished several lakes. Ray and I had not been in sheep country fifteen minutes when I spotted four rams less than three quarters of a mile away. One was a fine legal ram, but it wasn't the one I was looking for. I passed up the shot and gave it to Ray. The route of the stalk was absolutely perfect. A short time later, he killed the bedded the ram at a hundred yards.

Meredith and Tom were also successful. After Ray and I returned to camp, I was speechless when I saw two brook trout, more than seven pounds each. The largest was twenty two inches long and eighteen inches in girth. Never was there a more elated and jubilant hunting camp. We raised our cups to the mountains and the wildlife that inhabits them. It had been one of the most memorable days of my life.

September 22. We packed Ray's ram out of the mountains. That night, as I returned to camp alone, a spectacular, multi-colored display of northern lights danced in the sky. Even in my travels to Canada and Alaska, I had never seen such a pretty and active show.

September 23 - 30. Snow. Constant snow.

October 1. Snow. Late in the afternoon, the storm finally appeared to be waning. I quickly assembled a light camp and set out on foot for sheep country. The snow was wet and more than knee-deep. Elk season was open, and I passed several cows within a hundred yards as they pawed the ground for food. I declined to shoot one because I didn't want to ask my horses to carry the extra weight if the snow forced us to leave the mountains. Just as I reached sheep country, the snow clouds and blizzard again descended. I was already exhausted from wading in snow, but I turned around and started for base camp.

October 2 - 3. Snow. Although Meredith and I were snug in our tent with plenty of stove wood and food, the horses could no longer find enough to eat under the deepening snow. We pulled down our tent, packed our camp, and headed for the lowlands. A tough two days of wading through deep snow lay ahead of us. We crossed a high pass in a blizzard the first day. Dangerous rocks and bottomless snow pits were concealed under the drifts. The horses often bogged down in belly-deep snow and lunged for solid footing. At one point, I saw Meredith get down from her saddlehorse and examine one of the mare's front legs. As I approached, I saw that jagged rocks below the snow had snagged the horse's shin and that there was a scarlet trail of blood. We dressed the wound in silence, each of us feeling low and upset. We would rather hurt ourselves than our horses.

October 4. After tremendous effort, we finally made it down out of the highcountry. We and the horses were completely played out. The mountains had nearly been our downfall; we were exhausted beyond words.

October 19 - 29. The weather finally broke, and the snow settled and blew from ridges and slopes. I was determined to try a last time for a ram. My friend, Tim, and I spent two days traveling to the hunting area. I shot a dry cow elk for winter's meat, knowing this was the last trip of the season. While climbing to sheep country and clawing our way up an icy chute, I slipped and crushed my rifle scope. I was glad to have the insurance of iron sights on my rifle.

On a ridge in the heart of some of the most magnificent country on earth, Tim and I examined hour-old ram tracks in the powdery snow, while a gale wind froze our damp clothes. With our binoculars, we traced the tracks as they steadily climbed up, up and over a mountain. It was late afternoon of the last day of the hunt and useless for us to follow; my sheep hunt was over.

Was I disappointed at not shooting a ram? Not really. I had spent many weeks in sheep country during the summer and fall and had participated in two sporting stalks with hunters who had killed rams. My wife, my friends, and I had shared many star-filled nights and campfires. I had seen several handsome, legal rams and passed them up in hopes of finding an old ram. I had heard elk bugle, tasted icy glacial streams, listened to pikas and marmots call, and watched the snow filter through gray skies and settle on pine boughs. I had listened to young coyotes yip, marveled at the speed of diving eagles, given silent thanks to my patient horses, and studied the yellow and red leaves of autumn. I had found peace with the world and myself. No, I was not disappointed. Before Tim and I left the mountains, we paused briefly on an open valley floor far above timberline. Tall peaks towered on all sides, and the frozen landscape was as bleak and barren as the moon. The cold wind burned our cheeks and roared in our ears. I had to shout in order to be heard.

"Tim, all fall I've asked myself if it's worth it to hunt in this horse-killing, man-crippling country. But look at it," I yelled as I waved my hand in the direction of the rugged peaks with clouds of drifting snow racing off their tops. "How can I stay away?"

Tim's eyes flickered with understanding laughter as he looked from the peaks to me. He nodded, then continued on through the rocks and snow.

Chapter Eighteen
Success and Silent Partners

 Our elk-hunting adventure began in the Bob Marshall Wilderness of Montana during the fall of 1978. I worked for an outfitter there and happened to befriend one of the elk hunters, "Dead-Eye Joe" from some foreign country named New York. Joe was a man worth befriending, a dedicated sportsman, and deadly marksman. My new friend wanted an elk more than anything, but fate was cruel that year and Joe went home without having fired his Deathray 7mm magnum.

We continued to correspond during the next few years and hoped to hunt elk together again someday in Wyoming. Joe religiously applied for a non-resident elk license each year, but was continually unsuccessful in the draw. Meanwhile, he joined an expedition in Idaho whose purpose was to search every nook and cranny for that elusive trophy, the wily wapiti. The expedition flopped, and Joe again returned home empty-handed. The score now stood at elk - 2, Joe - 0.

Then one day, Joe nearly hugged his mailbox. With a Wyoming elk license in hand, he was ecstatic. In excitement, he contacted me and everyone else he could think of who knew anything about elk. He hungrily read every article he could find about the subject.

He began an exercise program. He made sure every item of his gear was perfect, and he spent many, many hours at the rifle range. His wife rolled her eyes back in her head and longed for hunting season to begin—and end. She is credited with the proverb, "Hunting is not a sport. It is a disease."

Joe and I ironed out the details, and finally the day arrived when I met him at the airport. It had been five years since we had hunted together in Montana, and we had much news to catch up on. If I ever saw anyone who suffered from city tension, hunt-preparation exhaustion, and excited anticipation, it was Joe. I knew the only cure was to rush him to the highcountry and let him fill his lungs with clean air and his eyes with views of unspoiled elk country.

The next morning, we packed the horses with a light camp, our personal gear, and as much horse feed as possible, then hit the trail early. We met a snowstorm at the trailhead, and I looked with amazement at another group of out-of-state hunters preparing to leave for the mountains with an outfitter. I guess they figured that anyone who is going to ride a horse should look the part. They were dressed in cowboy hats, blue jeans, and pointy-toed cowboy boots with no overshoes. There may be no worse combination of cold weather clothing; I shivered as I thought about the cold ride in store for those hunters. Joe and I, on the other hand, looked like two Eskimos perched on our horses as we started for elk country.

We arrived at our hunting area later that day and set up a basic but snug camp. The city tension and stress had been erased from Joe's face, and only a show of the keen delight of hunting remained. We walked from camp the next morning and sweated and puffed our way toward timberline long before daylight. The crusted snow crunched loudly underfoot. The sky was clear, cold, calm. At timberline, I glassed a mountainside a mile away where I thought a bull might be, and, lo and behold, there stood the king of the mountain himself, bugling off his six-point head. Highlighted by the sun's first rays, the bull was magnificent.

And Joe? Well, how can one describe the expression of a man who has lived, thought, and dreamed elk for years, traveled thousands of miles to hunt them, then sees a beautiful herd master bugling while driving a band of cows before him on a frosty mountainside? Even if we had turned around and gone home at that point, Joe said his hunt would have been worthwhile.

The stalk was tough. The big bull was with a number of cows and small bulls. They all began drifting down the slope toward the timber below. We had to try to cut them off, but were hampered by a shortage of time, cover, and more elk.

Several times, we saw other bands between us and the six-point bull, but none had a better bull with them. Joe, who had not seen a live elk on his two previous hunts, was now up to his ears in them. Hurrying to head off one bunch of elk while trying to not alarm others, we finally reached a vantage point at the edge of a draw where we expected the big bull to emerge. Joe got into a suitable shooting position for one of the most important shots of his life.

Into our view came a line of cows and calves. Cows, cows, and more cows—then the bull. The range? It was a fair piece. Although I was never an advocate of long-range shooting, Joe and I simply could not get any closer before the elk would vanish into the timber. I would have advised most hunters to let the bull go but, with Joe, I felt differently. Here was a hunter with a finely tuned rifle, literally a rock-steady rest, and much practice at targets from similar distances.

I whispered good luck to him and watched his shots. Only after the echoes had faded away and the bull lay upon the ground did Joe allow his near-bursting emotions to let go. He began to jabber like a wild man. It was a golden hunt, a fine trophy for a deserving and dedicated sportsman. Around the campfire that evening, we discussed and relived every angle of the hunt.

Not to steal the limelight from Joe but to give credit where it was due, I mentioned an important factor that contributed to the success of our adventure—our silent partners. Partners who may not have been on the mountainside with us, but nevertheless made the hunt possible. Partners like Joe's wife, who tolerated his addiction to hunting and wished him well while waiting for his return. Partners like my wife, who tolerated my addiction to hunting and helped in a thousand ways. Partners like my patient horses whose muscle and bone made the trip possible. Just as important, silent partners like the many dedicated, professional people of the state and federal wildlife management agencies, conservation organizations, and others who try their best to ensure that bull elk will always bugle from frosty mountain slopes. Yes, Joe actually had quite a crowd looking over his shoulder, if only in spirit, as he sighted down his rifle barrel that day.

Chapter Nineteen
Ram Tracks in the Snow

 I had been expecting Tim to arrive sometime before noon on a warm July day. I couldn't conceal my delight when his blue pickup finally came into sight over the sagebrush-covered hill. It is always good to see a friend, but Tim's visit had a special purpose. Though he had wanted to surprise me, I already knew what his mission was. I had found out through the grapevine that he had drawn a bighorn license. After dinner, he and I went out on the porch to visit while he had a smoke.

"I've got a problem, friend," he told me.

"You're one of the luckiest guys I know. How can you have a problem?"

"I drew a sheep tag."

I carefully hid my enthusiasm. "Shoot, that's no problem. You just finish your ranch chores and take some time off. Meredith and I will bring our horses over, help you get back to the hills, and look for a sheep. If you get one, we'll pack it out and you can eat it all winter. What seems to be the problem?"

Tim then revealed something I did not know. "My friend, John, drew a sheep license, too." This was a hold card I had not figured on.

"Oh," I said flatly.

We did have a problem because, as Tim knew, I was very reluctant to hunt with someone I did not know. I had seen too many slob hunters to want to go to the mountains with every guy who wore an orange cap. Tim also knew I was possessive about "my" hunting areas.

He and I read each other's eyes. I had met John a few times but was not well acquainted with him. I finally spoke. "What kind of hunter is John?"

Tim said the only thing he possibly could have said to put my mind at ease: "I hunt with him." He said a whole lot with those few words, and immediately I decided to help them with their sheep hunt.

Although the season didn't open until the first of September, Meredith and I went to the mountains around the first of August. We planned to explore new country as we worked our way over a mountain range, across a large basin, and into a second mountain range. In the second range was where we planned to help Tim and John hunt sheep. In the meantime, we had three weeks to do nothing but the things we loved most—explore the silent, empty places and forget about nuclear warheads, checking accounts, ringing telephones, and busy highways.

During the first day of our journey, we traveled only a short distance so as not to overwork our horses. They had much work to do during the coming weeks and we could not afford to injure any of them. We camped in a small clearing with exceptionally lush grass and a stream cutting through the middle of the meadow. How the horses loved that spot! They were more than happy to graze, rest, and graze some more on the rich, deep grass.

We decided to lay over a day to let the horses enjoy the meadow and to let us explore some of the immediate area. Late in the afternoon of the second day, I saw the horses suddenly throw their heads in the air. A medium-sized black bear was across the stream, walking straight toward us. The wind was wrong for it to smell us and the noise of the stream concealed any other sounds. The bear was oblivious to our presence, but was making the horses nervous. I walked toward the bear and shouted to get its attention. The bear came to an abrupt halt less than a hundred yards away and looked us over before he ambled away.

The next few days of our trip took us higher and deeper into the mountains. Our camps were in the heart of the majestic peaks that I had often seen at a distance. I had wondered what sights were contained within those peaks. During our trip, I found out. One clear morning, I stood at the edge of a gently sloping meadow covered with many kinds of wildflowers. To my left was a clear, fast-moving stream at the base of a towering, rocky peak. In front of me was a thick stand of timber. On my right were three rock ledges with several foaming white waterfalls spilling over them. Fresh elk tracks were embedded in the dirt of the meadow. I hoped heaven was like this.

It required several days to cross the mountain range and descend to the lower sagebrush country on the other side. After a long day's travel, we arrived at the ranch where Tim worked. He had been expecting us, and together we completed our plans. I was to return to the ranch after two weeks and help Tim and John pack into the mountains. In the meantime, Meredith and I would explore more new territory. We restocked our supplies and returned to the highcountry.

We took a cross-country route when we rode out of the ranch. By traveling through open spaces and using faint game trails in the timber, we finally reached timberline and worked our way into the mountains. From a high peak, we looked back across the valley we had crossed and saw the range of mountains where we had camped during the first week of our trip. We had traveled nearly sixty miles, but from our elevated position, we could trace a large part of our route.

Meredith and I rambled freely around the mountains. We didn't know what day it was or what time it was, nor did we care. During a layover day at one of our camps, I climbed a high ridge to explore and scout for game. I walked from camp fairly late in the morning and didn't expect to see any deer or elk. A few fresh tracks proved the animals were present, but were already bedded in heavy timber for the day. From a high, rocky knoll, I glassed what appeared to be the curl of a ram. My spotting scope revealed a dark-colored ram with large, heavy horns. I watched him as he got up from his bed and grazed on a steep hillside. An hour later, I returned to camp in high spirits.

The next day was Meredith's turn for adventure. She filled her daypack with snacks and camera, and left camp early. All day, she explored a remote basin that seemed to be a perfect paradise. When she returned to camp late in the afternoon, she excitedly told me about seeing signs of nearly every kind of animal that lived in those mountains—grouse, ducks, songbirds, ravens, fish, moose, elk, deer, mountain sheep, coyotes, and black bear.

Once she found herself in a clearing near a pretty, little lake only a stone's throw from a band of bighorn ewes and lambs. The sheep stared at her and then nonchalantly grazed away. My bride had enjoyed quite a day.

We traveled leisurely from meadow to meadow and camp to camp. The tentative destination was a fabled lake where, according to hot tips whispered in low tones, we could catch trout as long as our legs. Either someone had pulled our legs or we didn't find the right lake, because the only fish we caught where delicious pan-sized fighters.

Above one of our camps in a small, secluded valley, we made several interesting discoveries. Both Meredith and I found ancient, weathered buffalo skulls. Neither of the two skulls was complete, but the skull I found had the eye sockets, forehead, and both horn cores. The horn cores looked as if the horns had only recently slipped off of them. I continued to search the area and found the prize—both of the cracked and weathered horns. Buffalo had been gone from that area for almost a hundred years. We were amazed that the skulls and horns had lasted so long.

After nearly two carefree weeks, it was time for me to return to the ranch. Meredith remained with several horses at a meadow we would use as a base camp for Tim's and John's sheep hunts. I led a pack horse as I traveled from the mountains.

I had an unusual experience before I arrived at the ranch. Choosing to sleep out instead of reaching the ranch after dark, I found a suitable camp near a slow, meandering stream. Because the late August weather was still quite warm, I slept under a thick wool blanket. During the night, I was snapped out of a deep sleep by something in my bed moving over my bare feet. It didn't require much imagination to identify the intruder from its length and its cool, clammy scales as it slithered between my toes.

118   *Plains & Peaks*

In the span of one millionth of a second, I reminded myself that few rattlesnakes had ever been seen in that area, and that my cold-blooded bed partner was probably just a water snake. Harmless water snake or not, in the next millionth of a second, I jerked the blanket away and launched the snake with a much-inspired kick. I was relieved not to hear the angry buzz of rattles after the reptile thumped into tall grass nearby.

Things were hopping at the ranch when I arrived. Tim was frantically racing hither and yon, finishing all of his ranch responsibilities in order to take time off, and simultaneously preparing for his sheep hunt. I felt exhausted just watching him as he scrambled from pre-dawn to post-dark.

John arrived at the ranch during this turmoil and organized the food department of the hunt while sorting and stacking box upon box of food. It was clear we would not starve during the hunt. Tim's house became the headquarters for the expedition, and soon, piles of boxes, duffle bags, backpacks, panniers, tents, stoves, and gear cluttered the floors. It was enough to make a tidy housekeeper weep. Tim had borrowed several horses from the ranch to use for the hunt. I looked in horror at the two we planned to pack. They were good, gentle, stout horses, but were rolling fat from a summer of idleness—prime candidates for cinch galls and sore backs. We could only hope for the best.

Finally, we were ready and, in the early morning twilight, packed and mounted the horses. John humorously gave our battle cry: "Let's go smite those fuzzy suckers!"

"Tally-ho," I cheered.

Tim sat on his dancing roan gelding, his eyes flashing with excitement.

The day we packed into the mountains was one of those rare, absolutely beautiful days. No clouds, no rain, no snow, no wind. Our spirits were jubilant. Any doubts I harbored about taking John to the hills evaporated. He was like a child at a circus, constantly showing sincere delight at everything he saw. It gave me great pleasure to travel the silent trails of the mountains with someone who appreciated them as much as he did. I knew we would have an enjoyable, successful hunt, even if we did not see a single bighorn ram.

We arrived at base camp late in the afternoon and immediately pitched two canvas wall tents. Meredith cast hungry eyes on the panniers crammed with food and quickly carried an armload of groceries to the tin stove in the cook tent. The rest of us finished making camp and tending the horse herd. Soon, we had a rough but adequate base camp.

The day before sheep season opened, John, Tim, and I took a backpack camp near the area where I had seen the dark ram a few weeks before. Meredith agreed to watch base camp and the horse herd while we made our first foray into sheep country. We each carried our own bedroll, personal gear, and food. The three-man tent, gas stove, and spotting scope more than made up for the lack of a rifle on my pack.

We camped at the edge of a small clearing in heavy timber. Water was limited to a clear pool ringing the base of a large boulder. After pitching the tent, we climbed a small, rocky knob to look around and pass the time. Our concentration on the scenery instead of on scouting for game was nearly a bad error. Tim had barely sat down and raised his binoculars before he said, "I see a ram! He's staring right at us!"

There was little we could do but act nonchalant and stare back at the ram. He was a half-curl, too young to interest us, and was bedded on a grassy ledge of a rough, cliff-like slope above timberline. We eased to a more concealed position and watched the young ram for nearly an hour, during which he began to graze. We determined the sheep was alone.

At camp, just before dark, I strolled out into the clearing to fill a pan with water. As I stepped from behind a pine tree, I suddenly saw an exceptionally plump cow elk at the opposite edge of the opening. The cow spooked into the timber above our camp and began barking across the calm evening. We built no fire that night and tried to not disturb the neighborhood any more than we already had.

In the twilight of opening morning, we walked from the spike camp. Excitement charged the air. We combed the entire all day, yet failed to locate any sheep. Our day's tally included several bands of elk, a few grouse, a pair of golden eagles, and several promising fishing spots.

We passed an enjoyable day before retrieving the spike camp and descending the mountain. We voted to regroup and rest at base camp before making a second try for rams. By the following morning our group was fresh and eager. John stepped on to his horse and jested at the expense of some antihunting propaganda he had read, "Let's go blast great, big, bloody, gaping holes in those brown-eyed varmints," He turned his horse in behind the pack horse Meredith led as Tim and I brought up the rear on foot.

Our plan was to travel a few miles above base camp where Meredith would drop us off with our packs before returning to camp. John, Tim, and I would climb to new country and hunt for several days. Our plan hit a snag shortly after we left base camp. The pack horse carrying our backpacks decided he was homesick and scattered our gear for a remarkable distance on his way back to his four-legged buddies at camp. After repacking the horse we hit the trail again.

When John saw the mountain we would have to climb to reach sheep country, he suddenly lost his usual good humor, "My goodness, why can't the sheep live on the bottom of the mountain instead of on top of the silly thing?"

I felt he was acquiring a true appreciation and understanding of sheep hunting. Because it was only midday, Meredith decided to climb with us and traded off carrying the loads. Near timberline, the steep chute we climbed began to level off. We began to see old sheep sign as we looked for a suitable camp. Meredith returned to the horses and base camp while we set up our tent. With a couple of hours of daylight remaining, Tim and I decided to walk to a nearby ridge while John rested at camp.

Tim and I had not traveled a half-mile when Lady Luck smiled and winked at us. From behind a rock ledge, I spotted three rams feeding. Two of the rams carried horns past the legal three-quarter curl mark, but were not the record-book candidates Tim was looking for. We agreed one of us should return to camp and get John. Tim volunteered and raced back over the rocks like a wild man.

The three sheep seemed nervous. They alternated between grazing, resting, and milling in small circles. I am not sure what words Tim used to make John forget his fatigue, but soon the two nearly bounded over the rocks to me. The rams were bedded when John first looked through the spotting scope. He came away from the glass with a broad smile on his face.

The sun was near the western horizon. Because of the terrain and the constant nervous milling of the rams, we felt the chances of finding them in the morning was small. A stalk had to be attempted immediately. Tim reasoned that two people made less commotion than three and announced he would remain behind to keep watch on the rams while John and I stalked.

The temporary surge of adrenaline had exhausted itself in John's system and though his spirit was more than willing, his legs and lungs rebelled at every inch of the stalk. Adding to our difficulties, the only easy approach to the rams was blocked by fifty yards of open terrain we dared not cross. We were forced to flank the sheep along a series of short, steep knolls covered by large rocks and wind-stunted trees. We tried to balance the disappearing daylight with John's burning lungs and crept over and around the sheep knolls. Finally we overcame the many tricky obstacles and watched the wary rams from behind a clump of dwarfed pine trees nearly two hundred yards away. The proximity of the sheep started John's adrenaline flowing again, and he got an excited twinkle in his eye.

"Anytime you're ready," I reassured him.

Things looked good until John belly-crawled to a suitable position. The smallest ram saw the movement and froze. The other rams sensed danger and poised for flight. John carefully found a steady rest for his .270 rifle. I signaled the largest ram's location by holding up three fingers and pointing to the middle one. John nodded, then looked through his scope.

Before we left the ranch, I had watched John consistently hit targets with his .270 at various distances, but under much different circumstances than he faced as he aimed at the ram. Punching holes in paper targets is a lot easier than taking a quick shot at an alarmed ram when you are panting and tired. Yet John made a perfect shoulder shot, the result of not luck but of skilled and experienced shooting. The ram humped up, made a few quick leaps, and collapsed before the echoes of the shot faded.

I let out an excited yell to relieve my built-up tension and then congratulated John. The usually vociferous John was completely speechless, but beamed with joy. One of the toughest, most suspenseful, and challenging stalks I had ever participated in had come to an end. We walked to the ram and were joined by Tim. Together we admired the beautifully curved horns before gutting the ram. It was dark when we arrived back at our spike camp. A hot meal somewhat revived our tired muscles. With sleep impossible in our continued excitement, we indulged ourselves with the satisfying atmosphere of a small fire and talked about the hunt as we relived every cherished part of it. Much later, when we lay in our bedrolls in the small tent, John fairly summed the entire hunt, "Jack O'Connor surely smiled this evening from that great sheep range in the sky."

I thought about that for a moment before I fell into a deep sleep.

Time was running out for Tim. I had helped him look for a ram nearly the entire month of September, yet we still had not found the one he wanted. We had hunted hard. Around a campfire one evening, we estimated we had walked over eighty mountain miles and ridden an additional 150 during the search. Many days had been spent glassing miles and miles of mountains for a prize ram. Twice we had found rams, but none with what we were looking for. Tim turned down several legal rams, holding out for an older, well-broomed ram. I silently cheered his decision since I believed anyone who has walked away from a mediocre ram in the hope of finding an old ram is a serious, dedicated sheep hunter.

Our spirits never slumped. Both of us understood and cherished the privilege of hunting for a magnificent bighorn ram in the most spectacular terrain on earth. We realized the hunt was far more important than the kill. Tim's boss had reluctantly granted him an extension of time off from work. Tim painfully watched as his remaining hunting days approached the deadline. With time against him, he finally confided to me that he would consider any legal ram we found during the last days of his hunt. I knew it was a tough decision for him and did not torment him by questioning it.

For the final few days of the hunt, we packed our base camp to a new area. Unfortunately, we picked an exposed location for the canvas wall tent. During the night a howling blizzard swept the mountains and flapped the tent like a limp rag. Time and time again the tent stakes were ripped from the ground and left the billowing canvas in danger of taking off like a big white bird. Since sleep was impossible, I grabbed the upwind corner of the tent with my exposed arm and became a human anchor for the duration of the night.

Regardless of the restless night, Tim and I set out early the next morning to hunt a large basin a few miles above camp. The new snow was at boot-top level and exhausted us as we trudged through it.

By that stage in Tim's hunt I was used to the fact that he carried a minimum of ammunition, four shells in the magazine and one emergency round in his pocket. I had been astonished the first time I learned of his habit, so different than the "Gatling-gun" approach of many hunters. He explained if he fired all five shots and still had not killed a ram, then he did not deserve one. I started to protest but remembered the many shooting trophies Tim had won. A few years after our hunt together, Tim joined the Army and received top marksmanship honors in his company. His skill with light weapons helped earn him a green béret in the Special Forces. Five shells were enough.

We finally reached the basin and carefully worked our way to an observation point. Huge white clouds of loose snow were ripped from the peaks overhead by blast after blast of gale force winds. Tiny sparkles of snow glittered everywhere in the clear, cold sky. Our attempts to glass the area were frustrations and miserable. Each time we raised our binoculars toward the basin, icy winds would burn any exposed flesh and cloud our eyes with teardrops. Strong gusts physically rocked us despite our solid rests and made careful, detailed glassing impossible. We looked for tracks as much as for animals but failed to locate any sign. Shivering with cold, we finally decided to move from the observation point and comb several small draws in the basin which we had not glassed.

As long as we walked we stayed warm. Our rest stops and glassing sessions were limited by the icy wind penetrating our sweat-dampened clothes.

We paused briefly to eat our lunch near a small, ice-covered pond. I tried to break a hole in the already thick ice with the heel of my boot but was unsuccessful. We labored through the drifted snow of several draws and saw only the fresh tracks of coyote. By late afternoon, we had hunted the entire basin except for one small draw. The basin appeared empty of sheep, and the temptation to return to camp was great. For no other reason than the fact that it was more or less on the return route to camp, we decided to trudge up one more ridge and check the last draw.

A single trail in the snow caught my attention as we wearily crested the rim of the draw. We judged it to be the track of a coyote but walked up to it for closer inspection. With mixed feelings of joy and disbelief, we saw large, distinct ram tracks. The tracks, disturbingly fresh, were fading in the drifting snow even as we watched them. Tim removed the rifle from his shoulder as I quickly looked around. We nervously followed the tracks along a rugged, rock-covered ridge above a steep, almost cliff-like, south-facing slope. Not far away, the tracks joined other sets of ram tracks. The signs of feeding rams were only minutes old and were on all sides of us as we eased along.

Although it is enjoyably suspenseful to follow ram tracks so fresh that the rams have to be within rock-throwing distance, it has never been known as the best way to kill a ram. It was a fifty-fifty gamble that we would see the rams first. Even so, our best bet seemed to be to follow the tracks carefully and hope Lady Luck was with us.

Once again she smiled on us. I slowly peeked over the edge of the rimrock and saw two bedded rams less than a hundred yards below us. I eased back out of their sight, grinned at Tim, and signaled him to join me. Together we appraised the two rams.

Suddenly a third ram trotted past the bedded sheep and then a fourth ram materialized from among the rocks as if by magic. We continued to judge the curls of each ram as the wind swept past. Finally Tim picked the one he wanted, found a steady rest, and sent a bullet on its way. A heavy horned ram, bedded beside a large rock, never got to his feet as the other rams trotted away. I jumped up, stomped circulation into my numb legs, and gave a loud whoop that was carried away by the icy, cutting wind.

Chapter 20
Outdoor Stew

 I am often asked for my favorite outdoor recipe. It is a fairly simple one that is healthy and always a treat to prepare. Outdoors people rave about this old family recipe so I'll share it with you.

INGREDIENTS

1 complete habitat. 1 chilled morning. 1 - 4 humans (young ones are best). Glowing sunrise and sunset. A wide variety of wildlife. 1 small campfire with smoke.

1) Take one large expanse of untainted wildlife habitat and spread generously on the Earth's surface. There are many types of habitat to choose from. Some prefer the taste of salt water marshes blended with calm backwaters, others believe the quiet hardwood forests are more palatable, still others insist the flavor of rolling sagebrush and grasslands bring out the best. I am partial to the scent of pine forests mixed with the clear water of high mountain snow fields. It seems there are any number of habitats; all I have tried seem to work well.

2) Add humans to the habitat and blend them thoroughly until they absorb the texture and essence of the land. Place a rifle, shotgun, bow and arrow, fishing rod, binocular, or camera of choice in the hands of the humans. The final richness of the recipe is greatly enhanced if one or more of the humans are young and filled with the wonder of life.

3) Generously sprinkle the wide variety of wildlife on the habitat. There is no such thing as too much. The more diversity of species added the better. The best results are produced when the food chain is complete and balanced. Do not overlook the tiny insects or slimy creatures under rocks and in streams; it is easy to favor the large, fuzzy, brown-eyed fauna.

4) Mix together the habitat, humans, and wildlife well. Chill in a crisp morning sunrise. A red glowing sun creeping over the eastern

horizon adds much to the recipe. The mixture, like yeast, will become more active as the sky lightens and the temperatures increase. Marinate the humans in the spices of life, the sense of adventure, and a taste of freedom. Remember that the success of this recipe depends on how the humans react with the habitat and wildlife. If the young humans absorb the other ingredients and seem to grow, the recipe will be a satisfying success.

Continue to stir the mixture throughout the entire day. Often a fresh sprinkling of wildlife will renew the vigor of the humans.

5) Keep a close watch on the condition of the habitat and wildlife to make sure it remains plentiful and healthy. You may check the humans by turning them in the direction of their camp. If they move back into the mixture of habitat and wildlife, they are not yet done.

6) Just before sunset, place the humans around a glowing campfire. The smoke will add to the final flavor. A slight splash of alcohol may be added to the older humans if desired, but be careful not to add too much. Nothing will ruin your hard work of the day faster than a heavy hand with the alcohol. Slowly cool the mixture as the sun disappears. Billowing clouds in the background add a nice touch. Garnish the humans with any wild game or fish they have collected during the day. Dog hairs in the mixture from faithful retrievers or pointers are acceptable. Marshmallows may be added to the young humans at this time; you may expect some bursts of laughter during this process. When the sky turns black, generously sprinkle the heavens with the brightest of stars. After the campfire burns to coals, check the eyelids of the humans. If the eyelids appear heavy, roll the humans into warm bedrolls and let them season in the mixture overnight.

7) Repeat the recipe as often as possible - no one ever seems to grow tired of it. The recipe may be frozen in time and served at a later date by documenting the process with a camera. Some cooks embellish the original dish with exaggerated claims if served as leftovers. Enjoy!

Chapter Twenty-one
Third Time's a Charm

 It is said that the third time is a charm, and after my third sheep hunt, I am inclined to agree. Twice before, I had hunted bighorns for myself. Both hunts were extremely successful, and I even killed a ram on one of them. When I drew a third sheep license, I had no excuse but to be very selective in killing a ram. As with my second sheep hunt when I vowed to shoot an above-average ram or none at all, I again was determined to come home with an older ram, well past the legal mark. My third try for a ram had a different ending than had my second, when I finished the season without firing a shot.

I can't say I suffered any great hardship on that hunt. My hunting companion was also my favorite companion, my wife. Meredith helped me during the hunt in countless ways—organizing gear and food, packing horses, setting camp, cooking, glassing for sheep and, eventually, carrying meat off a rugged mountain. Good hunting partners are hard to come by, and no one needed to tell me how fortunate I was.

The August weather posed no threat to us. If anything, it was too hot. Unlike many alpine sheep hunts where wool pants and down parkas are the clothes of choice, light boots and T-shirts at noon proved to be the appropriate attire this time. Everything, it seemed, fell nicely into place. Blue sky, majestic mountains, willing horses, good company, comfortable camp, hungry fish in the creek flowing through our grass-filled meadow surrounded by proven sheep country. Certainly, life had been worse.

The trip to camp took most of the day. The ten-hour ride was pleasant enough, but man and beast alike were happy to arrive. Camp was a simple affair with only a small tent, a covered row of saddles on a convenient log, and a cooking area. The picketed and hobbled horses grazed a short distance away. It was well into the afternoon of the first day of hunting before Meredith and I saw any sheep. We had traveled that morning about five miles to an excellent sheep area. We spent the hiking to vantage points and carefully glassing every basin, each grassy spot, and all of the numerous rocky hiding places of bighorns. Then, late in the day, we hit potential paydirt. Only 900 yards away on a rocky ridge dotted with an occasional small wind-twisted pine trees, we started seeing sheep. We counted and watched rams as they quietly rested, slowly fed, and generally loafed on the long ridge. There were twenty five rams altogether, an impressive gathering by any sheep hunter's measure. What was not impressive was the size or age of any of the rams. Several carried legal three-quarter-curl head gear, but it was clear none were old rams. Most of the band appeared to be young sheep in the one-half-curl range.

I was disappointed that no old rams with well-broomed horns led the band. Nevertheless, it was quite a sight to see so many rams in one group and proved we were indeed hunting in likely sheep country. "In three or four years when those rams grow some more, there's sure going to be a lot of good rams around here," I said to Meredith.

"Yeah." she replied, "but where are the old rams today?" That was a good question. The following morning, we again set out from camp to see if we could answer it.

We worked our way slowly on foot into a high basin neighboring the drainage where we had seen the twenty five young rams. The small, clear stream that began at the basin's glaciers flowed into and out of three ice-cold lakes. Steep talus slopes and sheer cliffs rimmed the rocky basin. It was sheep country at its best, and we combed it slowly and cautiously with our binoculars.

The sun was at my back when I caught the telltale sight of small, white dots—rumps of bighorn sheep—moving slowly across a rockslide several miles away. A moment later, the spotting scope revealed eight rams grazing and ambling away from us as they looked for a place to lay down. The distance was too great to tell the exact size of the rams, but several showed horns that hinted of the length and heaviness of mature rams. We watched the group until it stopped, pawed beds on a steep, gravel covered slope, and began to lay down.

I glanced at my watch—10 a.m. "Let's hurry over there," I said to Meredith, who seemed as excited as I was. "I want to see some of those rams up close." We quickly gathered our gear into our packs and started toward the distant rams.

Our march took us down one side of the basin and up the other. The higher we climbed, the fewer shrubs, flowers, grass, or any kind of plant we encountered. By the end of our hike, we were completely surrounded by an intimidating amount of ice, jagged rocks, and cliffs.

It took four hours of constant hiking for us to reach the eight rams. Knowing it was vital for us to see the rams before they saw us, we slowed our pace to a creep during the last few hundred yards. Peeking over a ridge, I saw a single ram laying on a car-sized boulder several hundred yards away. No other rams were in view, but we knew they were probably somewhere very close. Meredith and I crawled together for a huddle and to make a plan of attack. We agreed that by dropping down a short distance, we would be

Outfitter Tory Taylor packs his own ram from the Wyoming wilderness

screened from the view of the single ram and could advance at least another hundred yards to a small rock pile. We started with all the speed of a lethargic snail. With each step, we paused to look for the hidden rams. Finally, we reached the rock pile, paused to calm our nerves, then peeked around washtub-sized rocks. Beginning less than a hundred yards in front of us, rams were sprinkled about on the gravel slope. The ram on the car-sized rock was the most distant, perhaps two hundred yards away. Some drowsy rams were bedded just seventy five yards from my .270's muzzle.

Meredith and I very slowly searched the rocks for rams and evaluated those we found. There were several better than one-half-curl rams. Most had legal three-quarter-curl horns. Two were above-average rams but were not broomed or old sheep. I still had not seen the ram I was hoping to find, but a quick tally showed there to be only seven rams. Where was the eighth ram we had seen earlier in the day? We laid behind the rock pile, watched, and waited for what seemed like days. The seven rams had no idea that I looked at each of them several times through my rifle scope as we waited. One ram got lazily to his feet and grazed a few minutes before again laying down. We noticed several of the larger rams would, from time to time, turn and look to a steep chute just above them. From our position, we couldn't see into the chute, but we had a hunch what it contained.

By that time, it was late afternoon and daylight was quickly running out. Camp was several hours away, across ankle-twisting loose rock. It was time for us to make a move. From behind the cover of the rock pile, we made a plan. In a moment, I steadied my rifle over a convenient rock, clicked the safety off and, a short distance below me, Meredith showed herself to the rams. Instantly, all heads snapped in our direction. Several of the large rams closest to us stood. Then, for an unbelievable, excruciating amount of time, nothing happened. The standing rams stared at us, turned their heads to the chute, again stared at us, and once more looked at the chute as if in question of what they should do. Finally, after what seemed like eternity to my fast-fraying nerves, all of the rams again laid down!

Watching a band of rams through my rifle scope as they intently watched me was nearly more than I could stand. Without taking my eye from the scope, I spoke to Meredith. "Walk toward them, but stay out of my line of fire." She took just two steps before all hell broke loose.

As Meredith began walking, all seven rams jumped to their feet. Suddenly, an eighth ram bounded from the chute and stopped for a split second in the middle of the closest rams. When he turned and saw Meredith and I, his eyes seemed to pop from their sockets. In the blink of an eye, he was racing away, shielded on all sides by the other rams. There was no way I could think about a shot, even as I heard Meredith shout "He's broomed way back on one side!" In the brief time I had to evaluate the eighth ram, I saw he was not exceptionally long horned, but was heavy at the half-curl mark. The tips of his horns seemed blunt, with one well broomed. He appeared to be an above-average ram, though not any record breaker. Quickly, I decided he was certainly good enough for me if a chance presented itself.

My hopes of getting a shot at the ram faded with each of his jumps. My heart sank as I watched them run away in a cluster. The old ram now had other rams on both sides, as well as at his heels. I could only helplessly watch him through my rifle scope. The rams were soon more than two hundred yards away. They approached the crest of a rock ridge and the safety it provided on the other side, when a miracle happened and the tables turned on the fleeing ram.

As I continued to watch through my rifle scope, the eighth ram suddenly turned from the others and jumped by himself onto a huge rock. He perched on the rock for a second, looked around briefly, then suddenly began to swing his head around to resume his escape. At that instant, the bullet from my .270 broke the ram's neck just in front of his shoulders. It was a quick, lucky shot, but a decisive one. The ram, dead instantly, rolled from the rock as the remaining seven rams disappeared.

The amount of time that lapsed from the moment we had first seen the eighth ram bound from the chute until the time I squeezed the trigger was only a few seconds—a short, action-packed few seconds, capping many, many pleasure-filled hours and days on that charmed hunt.

Chapter Twenty-two
Wily Wapiti

Early one morning, many years ago, I watched a fair-sized herd of elk perform a getaway maneuver from two hunters so calmly and smoothly that I still marvel at it. I was en route to help pack out a couple of bull elk killed the previous day by a friend and I. Stopping for a rest, I glassed a snow-covered mountain face a mile and a half away. The face rose at a moderate pitch from timberline and continued for a half mile to the crest of the mountain. Across the face, nearly fifty elk marched slowly, alert but not panicked.

The animals moved as one unit, led by a smart, wary cow. The elk at the end of the herd constantly covered the rear. Others on the fringes stared and listened in all directions. The animals walked cautiously several hundred yards above the protective trees, then suddenly stopped.

Through my binoculars, I discovered a hunter on horseback approaching the herd head-on from about four hundred yards and another horseback hunter trailing the herd at nearly the same distance. Neither hunter could see the herd on the curved face, but it was clear the elk knew danger approached from both directions.

From my ringside seat, I watched and waited, expecting any moment to see the hunters spring from their steeds and start piling up elk. The only elk that seemed particularly nervous was the lead cow. The others patiently awaited her decision. Above the herd was a small, well-used game trail leading to a low pass that the elk used frequently. I figured the elk would either break for the pass and expose themselves to the hunters near the top or stand where they were until the fast-approaching hunters discovered them. Instead, the lead cow gave a toss of her head and started walking, nearly tiptoeing, toward the timber below. The others followed in a calm, organized manner.

The last elk, a spike, must have just stepped into the trees when the trailing hunter topped the last rise and could see the area where the herd had stood just moments before. The timing of the herd's disappearance was uncanny. The hunters rode to each other, and I imagined their conversation:

"Seen any?"

"Nope. Have you?"

"No, but there sure are a lot of fresh tracks around here!"

The hunters finished their conversation, then continued on their separate ways, each following the horse tracks of the other and unaware of how close they had been to elk.

On another occasion, I received a different lesson about the keenness of elk senses. It was during an uncommonly hot day in August at timberline. I was hiking through basins filled with short willows, foaming brooks, and lush grass. I was scouting for deer and elk, and the fresh tracks of each told me I was in the right area. The shirt I wore as protection from mosquitoes was soaked with sweat. I walked at a fast clip with the idea of at least giving the biting bugs a moving target. I knew a slight breeze would welcome me at the high slope above.

I puffed up the last of a rise and quickly topped out. Immediately, I saw a dozen reddish-colored elk on a grassy knob five or six hundred yards way. They lay snoozing and loafing without a care in the world. A stiff breeze was blowing from me directly to the herd. Wondering what their reaction would be when my scent reached them, I began slowly counting to see how long it took the breeze to travel to them. I expected to see one or two of the elk lift their heads or stand; what happened was much more dramatic.

At the count of sixteen, the entire herd suddenly jumped to its feet and frantically ran for the nearest timber. It was as if a bomb had been dropped near the herd. I gained a lot of respect for the nose of an elk that day.

Elk are capable of covering a lot of ground—steep, snow-covered, rocky, or otherwise—when they have a mind to. Often, I have watched them run up, down, or across mountainsides with incredible speed, agility, and endurance. On many other occasions, I have watched elk move as quietly as cats.

I am still awed by the silent movements of a cow elk I watched from twenty yards away while bow hunting. I had been stepping from rock to rock up a small stream bed. On my right, the bank was covered with grass and, on the left, a stand of lodgepole pines sloped to the stream bed. I caught sight of a tawny movement and froze before watching several cows, calves, and a spike slowly walk across the timbered hill fifty yards above me. I was pinned down and exposed but motionless and undetected. One yearling cow, below the others, angled toward me, stopped to nip at a bite of grass, then moved past in absolute silence. If I had closed my eyes, I would not have known she was even there. After the elk grazed from the area, I walked the twenty steps to where the cow had grazed and, as an experiment, tried to walk the same route without making any sound. Pine needles crunched loudly underfoot, and I failed. It would have been easy to believe the cow's hooves had never touched the ground.

Like most animals, elk have a great ability to recognize danger and know how to avoid it. One fall, when I worked for an outfitter, I guided a father and son on a hunt. A small bunch of elk had stayed on a nearby mountain during that summer and fall. They had been near backpackers, fishermen, horse groups, and sightseers during the warm months, and had become accustomed to people's daylight schedules.

The elk also were hunted extensively each autumn and were very educated and wary. I concentrated on hunting them for a few days with the father and son, but with no results. From the fresh sign on our horses' tracks in the snow, it was easy to see the elk did not come out to the grassy parks to feed until after dark and faded back into timber before daylight. We tried following fresh tracks in the timber, only to have the crunching of snow spook the elk. It was a hopeless cause; we hunted in other areas for less wary elk and had much better success.

One of the biggest bulls I have ever seen killed was a hermit, too old to want the company of other elk. A hunter I was guiding broke the bull's thick neck with a single shot from twenty five yards. The hunter and I had tied our horses and stationed ourselves above a barren hillside. We waited for others of our group to join us, as a gale wind roared past. It was truly an unlucky day for the irregular seven-point bull, as he stepped into the open practically at our feet. We had chosen to sit on that hillside solely by chance; it was luck and not skill that had jinxed the bull's senses.

Although I learned that elk have keen ears, eyes, and noses and can run like the wind for miles if alarmed, I realized they had their weaknesses, too. One of those weaknesses is to be a creature of habit and use the same areas year after year. This made it possible to predict, sometimes with considerable accuracy, where elk were likely to be found. Once, I was shown a timbered ridge in Montana, one side of which dropped steeply several hundred yards to the bottom of a heavily forested draw. On the opposite side was a slope covered with lush grass, the best grazing for elk in the area. The outfitter for whom I worked at the time had for years posted hunters along the ridge with instructions to sit quietly and watch the grassy hillside. Every year, the outfitter's hunters took a few elk off this slope. During the hunting season that I worked the ridge, a magnificent six-point bull, big enough to squeak into the record book, was shot on the hillside from the often-used ridge.

An old, retired outfitter in Wyoming once showed me a box of empty brass cartridges he had picked up near his wilderness camp. The assortment of shells was amazing. The tarnished brass and several obsolete calibers showed the age of the spent cases. They had been found at the base of a chest-high rock overlooking a well-used pass between two major drainages. It was obvious that hunters had used the rock as a shooting bench for decades. The old outfitter could not even guess how many elk his own hunters had killed from the spot as the animals traveled from one drainage to the other.

Many years ago in Colorado, I discovered a game trail, primarily traveled by elk, so wide and well-used that I was astonished. It followed a bench carved by glaciers eons ago and connected two thick stands of timber. I never hunted the area nor met the hunter who parked his camper trailer a half mile away from the track-covered trail every year on the day before elk season opened, but I knew what that hunter was doing. He was taking advantage of the knowledge that elk frequently traveled the trail from habit and necessity because of the geography. How successfully he used the knowledge remained unknown to me, but I imagined he dined on elk steaks often.

An old friend of mine, gone now after seeing more than ninety winters, gave me a set of impressive, symmetrical, seven-point elk antlers before his passing. It was one of the last elk he ever killed and, during a hunting career of well over a half century, it was one of the larger bulls he had shot.

The story of the hunt for the bull was routine, seemingly uneventful, and not nearly as exciting as looking at the sweeping antlers. The old hunter had sat behind a large wind-fallen tree in the bottom of a wide, steep-walled stream bed. A small stream split miles of thick timber and was crossed by a game trail barely a hundred yards from the old man's ambush. He calmly killed the large bull with the same tactic, from behind the windfall, as he had used successfully for many years. He had discovered the spot after his failing hips demanded that the elk travel to him since he could no longer travel to the elk. Using his knowledge of the area and the habits of elk, my old friend found a place where the animals crossed frequently, and there he patiently waited. It was such a perfect setup that the elk usually woke the dozing old man as they kicked and rolled rocks in the stream bed.

Whether the hunting was hard or easy, I concluded long ago that there are few joys on earth so great as matching myself against the majestic elk. May they forever grace the land.

Chapter Tweny-three
Third Leg of a Grand Slam

 I fondly remember the first time I met Bob and the sheep hunt we took together a few months later. We met on a pleasant summer day during his short summer vacation. He had drawn a bighorn sheep license and had traveled from Louisiana to my neck of the woods to shop for an outfitter. At the time, I was working for a man named Brad, who was an avid sheep hunter, experienced outfitter and cattle rancher.

Brad called me from ranch headquarters and asked if I could come and visit with this prospective sheep hunter. Although the work is never done on a ranch, I had finished my morning chores at the ranch unit where I worked and had some slack time. I gladly grabbed my photo album and drove the twenty five miles to meet this hunter who was looking for an outfitter to take him sheep hunting.

Around the kitchen table at Brad's ranch, Bob, Brad, and I sipped iced tea and talked about wild sheep hunting in general and the bighorn sheep hunting in the nearby mountains, in particular.

I was immediately impressed with Bob. It was obvious that he was experienced, earnest, and thorough. He had already researched and memorized every scrap of information he could lay his hands on pertaining to his sheep-hunting area. He spoke of the area's hunter-success ratios, where most of the rams had been killed, what time of the season was the most productive, the average age of the rams taken, the average number of days each successful hunter had been in the field, and which drainages were the most productive. It was clear that Bob was a no-nonsense type of hunter who wanted a no-nonsense type of hunt. Evidently, Brad and I fit the bill. The day before sheep season opened that fall, Bob, Brad, and I packed our ponies and headed for the highcountry.

Before we started for the mountains, Bob made it perfectly clear that he had a dream. Like many others, that dream was to put a grand slam of rams on his wall. Unlike some, Bob's dream was much more than just idle talk or merely a wish to be part of the instant sheep-hunter crowd who wants only to kill sheep to boost their own egos. Bob's dream, like him, was sincere and honest. It made him a sheep-hunting purist, a true sportsman, and a mark above most hunters.

By the time he had drawn his bighorn license, he had already turned part of his grand slam dream into a reality by collecting two outstanding northern rams. His Dall ram carried forty-plus-inch horns; his Stone sheep made the record book. It has been my experience that talk is often cheap and the size of animal some hunters say they will accept on the first day of hunting is often much different and smaller than the animal they will settle for on the last day of hunting. Bob made us understand, in no uncertain terms, that he wanted a better-than-average bighorn ram or none at all. Period. I knew he meant it and hoped we could find such a ram.

This was the first time Brad and I had been together on a mountain hunt. With both of us serving as guides, we agreed to split the cooking, horse wrangling, and camp chores. Bob, always agreeable and helpful, pitched in whenever and wherever he could. His experience from other wilderness horsepack hunts was substantial and was put to good use. In no time, we had a smooth, efficient operation.

During the hunt, my eyes would pop open just as the eastern sky began to glow. Accordingly, I slept closest to the door of our canvas wall tent so I could get up to start breakfast without tripping over my companions, the collapsible tin stove, or our gear. While I performed my morning chef duties over an open fire outside the tent, Brad would tend the horses grazing on the frosted grass and Bob made lunches.

The evening schedule was slightly different. Brad was usually the evening cook while I tended the horses and Bob stood ready to help.

Our first camp was located at timberline on a sloping mountainside. The first rays of the morning sun would penetrate the clear, crisp air and cast long shadows on our campsite as we prepared for the day's hunting. Below our camp was a rugged granite canyon carved by glaciers once hundreds, perhaps thousands, of feet thick. The canyon was enormous with an equal amount of bare-rock outcroppings and scattered patches of fire-killed trees. Bighorns found the canyon to their liking, and hunting them in it was like looking for a needle in a haystack.

During the next few days, we spent hour upon hour glued to our binoculars and spotting scopes. A few bands of ewes and lambs showed themselves, but we could not locate rams.

One day, we were perched on the rim of the canyon. The wall of the canyon sloped steeply away to the river far below. To our left, the wall was thickly covered with yellow and orange aspen. Twenty five or more ewes and lambs suddenly appeared from a brushy draw and grazed slowly toward us.

Aware of our presence, they showed no fear. Several lambs frolicked, sprang onto every rock they passed, and pushed each other with their fuzzy, hornless heads, mimicking the battles that someday would be real.

After several days of dry runs trying to locate rams, the weather took a turn for the worse. The morning sky was filled with thick dark clouds, rain and snow alternately falling from them. Our prospects for finding rams that day were as dim as the sun's light attempting to penetrate the clouds overhead. We held a war council and decided to move camp to another location.

By late afternoon, as we set up our second camp, the clouds were thinning, and our thoughts and conversations turned to the next day's hunting.

When I become completely submersed in hunting, a normally dormant sense comes to life. Call it the hunters' sense, if you will. It hones the other senses and activates an inexplicable, innate biological barometer. In me, this barometer works in the form of a gut feeling that gauges the proximity of the game I am hunting. If I am close or traveling toward something worth seeing, often my barometric gut feeling tells me so. If I am wasting my time by hunting in the wrong area, then my hunter's sense seems as cold as a month-old track. I also believe prey animals possess a similar sense, which sometimes makes them become uneasy and exceedingly wary for no apparent reason.

On the day after we moved camp, Brad, Bob, and I rode our saddlehorses far up a drainage. The drainage was several miles long, filled with numerous trout-filled lakes and streams and, at its head, contained rocky basins sprinkled with alpine grasses. On countless occasions, I had watched rams feeding, resting, or moving through the basins. It was one of my favorite places to hunt for bighorns.

Near sheep country, we tied our three saddlehorses and continued on foot. From every suitable point, we would glass and glass for a telltale curl of horn, patch of hair, or distinct white rump. The entire time we walked and glassed, my hunter's sense kept pulling me on, giving me a gut feeling that something of interest was in the basins.

By late afternoon, our eyes felt the strain of combing every square inch of thousands of acres of sheep country. Still, we had seen no sheep. Then, from behind a four-foot-tall rock ridge that we used as a rest for our binoculars and spotting scopes, my gut feeling proved true.

"I see a sheep, a ram," I whispered, though the sheep I had spotted was more than a mile away. "There's another. Three. Four."

Most of the rams were bedded on what appeared to be a narrow ledge a short distance up a rock face. Through our spotting scopes, we noticed a fifth ram, as he nipped at short grass, just below the others. We sized the rams as they turned their heads to scratch their whithers with their horns or look lazily around for danger.

Our conclusions were somewhat disappointing. Most in the band were legal three-quarter-curl rams, but that was all that could be said of them. None were above average like Bob had wanted. It went without saying that we would not kill a sheep from this group of rams. We watched the sheep and glassed for others until shadows covered most of the mountains, then carefully retreated so as to not disturb the resting band of rams.

That evening at camp, talk over our supper plates contained a renewed sense of excitement. We had tried a new area, we had found rams, and we had many other excellent prospects to check during the coming days. The following day, we climbed to a high ridge far above timberline and glassed as a crisp wind blew through our sweat-dampened clothes. Although our noses ran and our bodies shivered, we continued combing the surrounding terrain with our binoculars and spotting scopes for several hours. We again found rams, but again none were above average. The day had drained our energy, and we wasted no time getting into our snug bedrolls after the supper dishes were washed and put away.

The next morning, I screwed up. We left immediately after breakfast and walked toward the same high ridge we had hunted the previous day. My hunter's sense continued to draw me to this area, and I harbored the feeling that somewhere on that ridge there was something worth seeing. It was a beautiful day. We inspected a large area that had been pulverized when a black bear dug for squirrel caches of white bark pine nuts. A short time later, we suddenly smelled the musky scent of elk and heard snapping timber. We froze motionless in our tracks as a cow elk trotted to within ten yards of us. For several minutes, she listened, sniffed, and stared back toward the area where we had jumped the herd of elk and had heard their noisy escape.

The excitement of seeing the cow elk at so close a distance still occupied my thoughts a few minutes later as we walked from the heavy timber just below a steep hillside covered with lush grass, scattered trees, and large boulders. I was in the lead. As I stepped from the heavy timber just at treeline, I glanced up to see a large ram racing away from us! We had reached sheep country by one short step, and I was caught flat-footed and unprepared. So much for being in tune with gut feelings. By our moving too quickly and noisily, the ram had been alerted before we ever saw him.

I vented my surprise with a few choice cuss words before quickly telling Bob to get ready to shoot. While Bob scrambled for a shooting rest, Brad and I tried to size the running sheep. The ram was perhaps two hundred yards away and running sideways to us. A glance at the ram through my binoculars revealed heavy horns with some brooming.

"He's better than average," I told Bob. "Take him if you want him." Brad gave a nod of agreement.

While Bob quickly squirmed into shooting position behind a small rock and looked through his rifle scope, the ram turned directly away from us and continued to leap up the slope. I silently continued to swear at myself and at Bob's impossible situation. This lone ram had shown us the penalty for not obeying the saying, "expect the unexpected." He had been in an area most suitable for elk; we had only taken one step into country where we could even begin to look for sheep. Literally in mid stride, Bob was forced to hit the ground, chamber a cartridge, and try to make a shot in a split second's time at a moving target. There was no time to evaluate the ram carefully, plan a stalk, or take that extra few seconds to steady the breathing before the trigger is slowly squeezed.

Shooting situations like this may have been common with automatic weapons during jungle maneuvers in Vietnam decades ago, but have never been the method of choice for sheep hunters. Bob's bullet zipped past the right side of the ram and drilled a ten-inch white bark pine tree squarely in the center. We never saw that ram again.

We were rattled. We spent more time than really necessary combing the area for any sign of clipped hair or specks of blood. There were none. After some time, we slowly and thoughtfully walked to a nearby rocky knob to glass during the afternoon.

By the following day, we shook off the remaining despair of jumping the large ram. During the morning, we combed another area using extra care not to stumble onto sheep. Bob took time in the afternoon on our way back to camp to catch some beautifully colored trout from a crystal-clear stream. The small collapsible fly rod was like a magic wand in Bob's skilled hands, as his well-presented flies drew the dark forms of trout from the bottom of pools.

One of my pleasures of life include watching an angler of Bob's talents work a stretch of pristine water. It's a thing of beauty. I truly believe that the afternoon did much for our spirits. We were reminded that to be free human beings happily pursuing our love of the outdoors is a precious blessing, one that cannot and should not be suppressed by thoughts of bad luck and missed rams.

Time was running out. On the last hunting day before we had to leave the highcountry, Brad stayed in camp while Bob and I tried once more to locate rams. Bob's ability to spot game was excellent. To be able to glass miles and miles of rugged country and identify a dot as a sheep from among the thousands of dots that are rocks is an art that not all people can master. As we sat on a ridge near timberline and glassed, I was not surprised when Bob suddenly announced that he saw a sheep. I quickly zoomed the sheep closer with my spotting scope. Three rams were restlessly grassing on a steep, bare mountain face terraced with narrow ledges nearly a mile away. Two of the rams were small; the third one was a ram that I can close my eyes and remember the sight of to this day. Soon after Bob spotted the sheep, the largest ram laid down on a grassy ledge, fully exposed. The bedded ram faced us and took our breath away as we looked at his exceptionally wide, deep curling horns. The ram was a classic.

Looking at him from the side, he was nothing worth writing home about. Long horned, yes. Heavy, yes. Well past the three-quarter-curl mark and better than average, yes, but still nothing to cause the blood pressure to rise— until the ram looked directly at you. The width of the ram's horns were more than impressive and made the ram as regal as a crowned king. In a few moments, Bob and I agreed that the ram was one that we wanted and plotted a route to him. The distance to the rams was not far and, since they had just laid down in the warm morning sun to digest their breakfast, we felt confident and fairly smug. The entire set-up looked like a piece of cake. I was already looking over the area to see how close we could take horses in order to pack out the ram.

Then our luck changed; something went wrong. Perhaps the ram's sense of danger gave him the gut feeling to move, perhaps we unknowingly spooked animals that, in turn, spooked the rams, or maybe the rams just plain did not like the view. In any case, we watched with despair as they suddenly got to their feet and briskly walked away.

Our hopes popped like a balloon poked with a pin. After the rams disappeared behind a rocky mountain, Bob and I quickly followed them and carefully searched the area. Nothing. Not even a glimpse of the rams or a fresh track. The wide-horned ram had vanished and taken our spirits with him.

The following day, our time was gone, and we had to leave the mountains. Bob had seen two large rams, but still was empty handed. There was nothing I wanted more than to help this extraordinary sportsman collect a ram. There was nothing more Bob wanted to do than to keep trying. We made plans to return in a few weeks and try again.

❦

By the time Bob returned for a second try, winter had set in to the mountains. The highest peaks were smothered by two feet of heavy, crusted snow. All of the hoofed animals—elk, deer, and bighorn sheep—had moved down to lower elevations for forage. Not a game track of any kind remained in the high mountains.

Taking a light camp on two packhorses, Bob and I rode from the ranch and headed for sheep winter range. For several days, we searched for rams and, instead, found many bunches of ewes, lambs, small rams, deer, and elk. Finally, we decided to move camp again to another drainage.

To reach the new drainage, we had to climb far above treeline before finding a break in a long cliff where we could descend with the horses. I knew the climb meant several grueling uphill miles of deep snow for the horses. On the morning we broke camp, I saddled my best saddlehorse and hoped the gray gelding was horse enough to get us over the top.

The gelding was an eager worker, full of energy, and normally walked at a fast pace while wanting to break into a jogging trot. As we worked our way higher up the mountain and deeper into snow, I decided to let the gelding climb when he wanted, rest when he wanted and, if need be, call it quits and turn around if he wanted. It was his call. I was not going to kill a horse just to get over the mountain. I leaned over my saddle and whispered to the puffing horse, "If you can get us up to the top of this hill, old buddy, that would be great. I know it's a heck of a pull. If you think we can't make it, that's O.K., too. I'll understand." As if the horse understood each of my words, the sweating animal flicked an ear back toward me, then ahead, looked up the steep mountain slope, then seemed to surge ahead with a determined will. I sat quietly in the saddle in appreciation and watched him work.

Later, when our pack string slugged through the last deep drift at the summit of the slope and stood resting and panting with the gray gelding at the lead, I made a silent vow that I would take as good of care of that horse for his entire life as he had kept care of me.

Bob and I immediately began seeing sheep. Numerous times, we stopped and glassed bighorn bands, hoping one of them contained the prize for which we searched. By the time we found a suitable camp and were settled, the day was drawing to a close. In the area where our camp as located, dozens of songbirds lived. I did not know what kind of birds they were and never saw one during our stay there, but heard their clear, peaceful chirps at dusk and dawn.

The following morning, we rode from camp ready for anything, but were totally unaware that the day was the one we had been waiting for. After leaving our saddlehorses near timberline, we worked our way into a burned area on the side of a rocky canyon. Three times within the next few hours, we saw rams. The first was alone, a young ram with not quite legal horns, moving quickly down the canyon. The ram passed without ever knowing of our presence. The second sighting was during one of our frequent glassing sessions when Bob suddenly said, "Possible Bingo. I see some rams way over there."

The rams were well over a mile away. We watched them feeding and resting before determining that none of the legal rams in the band were above average. We moved on.

On a rock knob where we paused to look things over, I spotted three rams walking slowly, several hundred yards below. I spoke softly to Bob and pointed toward the sheep. "There are some rams down there we had better get the spotting scope on." A moment later, I focused on the well-broomed, exceptionally heavy horns of one of the rams and quickly said, "There's your ram." Bob needed but one glance to agree.

We began working our way toward the animals and watched them walk out onto a bare-rock ledge, then lie down. The stalk, the one for which we had worked and waited so long for, then defied the laws of time. The next minutes seemed to fly past like doves on the wing while, in another sense, drag by with the speed of a glacier.

As Bob steadied his rifle, I swear the large ram looked quickly in our direction and seemed to burn holes through us with his stare. I nearly burst with anticipation before the silence was shattered by the roar of Bob's rifle. My blood pressure did not decrease when the ram leaped to his feet and began to race across the rocks! Bob continued to shoot, the ram continued to streak away, and I continued to approach the advanced stages of a nervous break-down and coronary failure.

The big ram went down, but instantly jumped back to his feet and kept running, though slower. Then, with another shot, I thought I saw hair fly from the ram. I saw Bob reach for his pocket for more shells and watched in horror as his hand snagged on his shirt, ripping the cartridges from his grip. Precious ammunition sprinkled like brass rain on the granite stones. Both Bob and I grabbed for still-rolling cartridges and got one chambered in the rifle just as the ram suddenly collapsed, thrashed briefly, and then laid still.

That evening, I silently echoed the sincere, heartfelt prayer Bob offered to God in thanks for all of our blessings received. During the following year, Bob traveled to Mexico where he finished his grand slam of North American sheep with a record desert bighorn. The total combined score of his grand slam placed it among the best ever taken. It was an honor to have hunted with such an outstanding sportsman.

Chapter Twenty-four
The Taylor Tribe Hunts Colorado Elk

 When the Taylor Tribe gathers, it's an impressive and bustling affair. The call went out; the clan was to rendezvous at our favorite Colorado hunting grounds and sponsor a family reunion around an elk hunt. The message triggered a complicated series of events involving much telephoning, letter writing, big-game license applications, conversations with travel agents, appointments with brand inspectors and veterinarians to obtain the necessary permits to transport horses interstate, and requests to employers for vacation time. The time, energy, and excited anticipation spent organizing this gathering would compete with the organization of a presidential inaugural parade.

Finally, the time arrived for the trek to our mountain mecca. Like iron filings drawn to a magnet, the Taylors gathered. The final tally was fifteen people from Montana, Wyoming, Colorado, New Mexico, and Nevada, all converging on the Colorado highcountry. Fifteen people gathered at a family reunion may seem rather unimpressive by some standards; on the other hand, fifteen people getting together to fill two elk licenses is definitely overkill.

Only two licenses? Yes, the Colorado Division of Wildlife's computer seemed rather stingy during the draw, but you can't argue with a machine. Dear ol' Dad and I were the chosen ones.

Until the night before the hunt, I was jubilant at the thought of being able to carry a rifle. Only then did I realize in what a tough spot I had put myself. Here was I, the one who always preaches a one-shot kill, the one who believes in hunting skills and sporting stalks, the purist who advocates doing it properly so that animals do not suffer, surrounded by the toughest bunch of critics and peers on earth. How could I withstand the pressure of half a dozen friends and family members looking over my shoulder as I aimed at an elk? What if I flinched and botched my moment of truth? What kind of example would I set for the younger hunters of the clan? As I laid in bed a few hours before the hunt, I said a little prayer: "Please, if I get a chance at Wily Wapiti, make the bullet fly straight. See to it that I don't stick my barrel into the mud or do anything unsportsmanlike. Mainly, make sure I don't wound an animal or I will expect the same treatment when I get to the end of my trail. Thanks."

I was the first of the vanguard to arrive at the Hardgroves' cabin, our base of operations for more than a quarter of a century. It was a Thursday, and it had taken me all day to trailer two of my horses from Wyoming.

What a beautiful day it was for traveling across the high plains and through valleys flanked by rugged peaks. I was following the heels of a snowstorm and admired the many landscapes it had decorated in white. I saw antelope and rabbits, horned larks and golden eagles, ducks and geese, deer and, of course, magpies and ravens picking scraps of unfortunate creatures off the asphalt. At sunset, as I traveled along the last leg of the journey, I paused to watch two proud, four-point buck mule deer approach a group of does and fawns grazing in a hay meadow. The meadow bordered a rock-filled creek and was surrounded by towering cottonwood trees still clinging to their bright yellow leaves. In the background stood massive, snow-covered, 14,000-foot peaks cloaked in dense timber. Above the peaks swirled a layer of white, gray, and pink clouds in a blue sky. The scene struck me as a good omen of the hunt to come.

On Saturday, Dad and I were in the saddle long before there was any sign of morning. Somewhere on the trail ahead, three brothers and a close family friend traveled on foot. I knew our horses would overtake them before we reached our chosen hunting area. As we climbed toward timberline, the eastern sky gradually filled with light. Darkness was finally replaced by a beautiful, clear day, enabling us to identify objects several hundred yards away. An intriguingly fresh, large elk track crossed our path and climbed the hillside above us. As we met the others of our group, we decided to tie the horses and continue with them on foot.

Crunch, crunch, crunch. To think we stood a chance of sneaking up on an elk was wishful thinking, but knowing they were not going to come to us, we hoped for the best. The crusted snow was taking a toll on Dad; we agreed to split our group. Dad, little brother, and our friend were left to stand guard on a large park. Although the park showed no fresh elk tracks that morning, we had shot numerous elk in it during previous years. It seemed as likely a spot as any, and we hoped it might once again be the right place.

Other than the single fresh track we had seen, elk sign in the timber was discouraging lacking. From past experiences, we knew elk often fed on the windswept slopes far above timberline when deep snow covered the ground. Two brothers and I started walking toward the distant alpine slopes. The precious minutes following daylight, the bewitching hour when elk sometimes linger in the open for a final nibble of grass, were rapidly disappearing. Leading the way, I set a grueling pace that soon had us wheezing in sweat-soaked clothes. Near timberline, the snow deepened, the air thinned, and three figures chugged upward, puffing like locomotives.

With a sideward glance through a narrow opening of trees, I saw an elk grazing on a distant slope. I froze in midstride, automatically reaching for the binoculars around my neck. By standing in place and swaying from side to side, I could see other elk, one a fair-sized bull. My brothers, a step behind, couldn't see the animals. A single step ahead, the view of the herd was also blocked by trees.

A moment later, following a brief pow-wow, one brother retraced our snowy backtrail to advise Dad of our sighting. My oldest brother and I continued on to timberline, then approached the herd by a lengthy, horseshoe-shaped route.

The elk were scattered on the windswept face of a rolling, grassy mountainside. In addition to the medium-sized bull we had seen earlier, a second large, heavy-beamed bull grazed among the herd. As we watched him from a half mile away, the large bull grazed away from the herd, climbed over a snow-filled pass to another drainage, and out of this story. Since that moment, I have lost considerable sleep wondering if that bull's antlers were even larger during the next hunting season and if he died of old age in the Colorado highcountry.

We lost sight of the herd as we neared the wind-swept face. The sun had climbed well into the sky, the bewitching hour long gone. A fear and disappointment of being too late hung over me, and disturbing questions raced through my mind. Where were the elk? Had they already moved into the timber? Had we unknowingly spooked them?

Suddenly my questions were answered. I saw movement at the crest of a rise four hundred yards away. My binoculars were up in a flash, and through them I saw the head of a cow elk running hard. My first thought was that she had heard our crunching steps and was running away. Then I saw she was running directly toward us. At the same instant, several more weaving heads bobbed into sight behind the lead cow. I dropped to a sitting position in the snow, chambered a round, and through the scope saw the flashing antlers of the medium-sized bull rocking above the trotting elk. To say the elk were running rapidly toward us would be an understatement. We were in the path of a crashing, leaping, awesome avalanche of elk.

The snow rooster-tailing from their pounding hooves sent a sun-glittering mist high into the air. The noise of snapping sticks as the stampede smashed through a willow patch was startling in the previous silence of the morning. The panicked herd leaped down a hill in flying, rabbit-like bounds. In the blink of an eye, they were upon us. They turned into a scattering of wind-stunted trees, and suddenly stopped. The morning was again silent except for the noise of the softly panting elk, rapid puffs of their steaming breath rose into the air.

A discouragingly small patch of the bull's shoulder was visible to me as he stood behind the thick limbs of a spruce tree. It was a tough shot, but more promising than one at a speeding, jumping elk. I settled the crosshairs and squeezed the trigger. The blast from the rifle started the elk running toward the nearby heavy timber. The bull humped with my shot, but ran as if uninjured. To aim at the bull was like aiming at a bouncing ball, but the second shot again gave the sound of a bullet hitting flesh. The bull continued to charge downhill like a runaway freight train. As I looked for a third shot, I saw a red blotch behind the bull's shoulder and lowered my rifle. The bull took several more ground-gaining leaps and suddenly collapsed in midair.

By Tuesday, I was once again alone at the cabin. The process of assembling the hunt was now reversed. The Taylor tide ebbed, and I was left alone to relive the treasured moments of a perfect hunt.

I sat in front of a popping, glowing fire radiating warmth and tranquillity from the stone fireplace of the century-old cabin. I reflected upon all the months of planning and preparation, rewarded in the few fleeting seconds when the elk appeared on the rise and ran toward my brother and me. I remembered the feeling of family closeness as a father and four sons packed the bull's quarters and antlers on the gentle, strong horses before starting off the mountain. I relived the exciting moments at daylight the following morning when Dad came within a hair of also killing a bull as he and I watched five bulls escort a score of cows and calves down a grassy, windy ridge just out of rifle range.

The hardwood rocking chair creaked in front of the cheerful fireplace as I sipped a cup of steaming cocoa and reflected on twenty five years of hunts, triumphs, and failures that took place outside those cabin walls. The surrounding mountains held memories far greater in value than all the gold taken from them.

Chapter Twenty-five
South of the Border Again

 The winter of 1992 found Meredith and I exploring Mexico again on the Baja California Sur peninsula and discovering for ourselves the wonders of that unique land where the desert meets the sea. Our forays included walking along pristine, sea shell-covered beaches as huge waves pounded their sands; snorkeling over ocean bottoms covered with plants and animals beyond description; night-paddling in sea kayaks through the glowing green mystery of bioluminescence where fish flashed through the sea like tracer bullets and water shot from our paddles like flames of green fire; and the once in a lifetime experience of reaching from a Mexican fisherman's ponga and repeatedly petting the fifty-foot bulk of a gray whale and her calf. Our wanderings also carried us inland to the unbelievable roughness of the volcanic plateaus and canyons, sparsely inhabited by plants tenaciously grasping life.

We were fortunate enough to witness some trees and cactus bloom for the first time in years after the break in the decade-long drought. Some travels led us to the homes of the sincere, gracious people of the Baja as well as to many of the old missions of the seventeenth and eighteenth centuries. Many of these churches still stand today as the hub of numerous towns and villages along the old Mission Trail that led from the tip of Baja northward more than 1,000 miles to the California missions at Monterey and San José near San Francisco.

The interior of the south Baja peninsula contains some of the harshest desert country in the world. Within the Baja's dry, cactus-covered boundaries lie beauty beyond belief, fascinating wildlife, rich human and geologic history, and a breed of unique Mestizo people barely scraping a living from the unforgiving desert.

I probably will never be able to hunt desert bighorn sheep due to the cost, but that didn't prevent me from visiting the rough home of desert rams and seeking traces of information about them. Everywhere I went in the Baja, I inquired about desert sheep and asked if they still could be hunted in Mexico. Many old men assured me wild sheep still lived in the remote mountains of the Baja, but none, it seemed, had seen one in many years.

I knew that somewhere on the Baja wild sheep must survive. In much of the peninsula I visited, however, the desert bighorns had been rubbed out or their existence hung by a thread. It appeared that teaching the principles of wildlife and habitat management had not been a priority of the Spanish Conquistadors or missionaries when they imposed the Old World onto the new one.

On one adventure, we drove to a small village to explore the wonderful cave paintings we had heard about. The road we traveled had recently been carved on the steep sides of volcanic canyon walls of an interior mountain range. With its abandoned vehicles along the shoulders, infrequent maintenance schedule, and blind corners on rutted, one-lane widths, the road would have been classified as a moderate four-wheel-drive road in the United States. By Mexican standards, though, it was a modern highway, a link to the world to be driven at high speed in any vehicle that was capable of turning a wheel.

The mountain village at the end of the road was a classic one: A random scattering of huts built from every type of construction material known to mankind; a timeless stucco church that could have been forty or four hundred years old; tremendous goat herds always accompanied by noisy, small children; and handsome mules and shaggy burros, some with white patches of healed saddle galls. In a glance, I knew we were in a place where people still depended heavily on the use of riding and pack animals. I felt as if I had just come home to a place I had never been before.

Our first order of business was to hire an outfitter/guide to take us into the canyons. In an effort to prevent vandalism and generate income from tourists, visitors to the cave paintings were required by the government to hire a local guide to accompany them. Our search for a guide first took us to the home of the village headman where protocol, custom, and the Mexican way of doing business dictated that we negotiate with this "mayor" before being assigned a guide. The negotiations took place in the headman's small kitchen/dining room/living room with a generous amount of fresh ground coffee, laughter, and visiting.

Sometime during this ceremony, a single, rough-looking rider appeared outside the fenced yard, mounted on an equally rough-looking unshod mule. The rider, dressed in the Mexican version of the latest Western cowboy garb, reined the mule to a nearly sliding stop with a severe, silver-inlaid spade bit before casually draping a leg over the swells of his ancient, weather-cracked saddle and exchanging pleasantries with the headman and his wife.

I was mesmerized by the trappings that the mule man wore. The spade bit was attached to a headstall comprised of braided rawhide, mulehair and hand-tanned leather. His Western stock saddle was of a vintage of many years past. A dirt-colored rag of a saddle blanket peeked from under the saddle skirts. The foot gear of the rider carried the trademark of the area's horsemen and villagers. Attractive, yet practical, low-cut, laced shoes made from homemade goat leather and treads from vehicle tires graced the feet of every man, woman, and adolescent in the vicinity. The only difference between the rider and his fellow villagers was that his shoes showed the signs of long, hard use. On the heels of his shoes were strapped handmade spurs with enormous rowels, the kind for which Hollywood costume directors would drool. The toe of the shoe was hidden by the protective shell of the stirrup's tapaderos. Just above the shoe, from the ankle to the knee, the rider had on armaderas, or armas, the equivalent of a leather gaiter, which protected the man's lower legs from the ever-present cactus spines along the trail. Covering the rider from hip to toe was a large, heavy leather apron. This arma was unique to the thorny, tall cactus country of Mexico. The leather piece was not worn like chaps of the North American cowboys, but instead was draped over the saddle horn and wrapped around the legs after mounting. From the waist down, the mule man was as protected from his thorny environment as a knight in armor.

The mule man soon finished his visit and spurred off on other errands. Shortly, we, too, finished our business with the headman and departed to find an overnight camp and prepare for an early-morning departure with our guide. When we asked about a place to camp, the headman showed us our options with a grin and a wide sweep of his hand in the direction of ten thousand square miles of empty Baja desert.

A heavy frost covered everything on the village's plateau at daylight the following morning, a surprise considering the groves of palm trees and orange orchards only a few thousand feet in elevation and a dozen miles below. Breakfast consisted of hot oatmeal and coffee cooked over the hiss of our gas stove. My meal was interrupted by the approaching tingle of burro bells and sharp shouts of a rider. I watched with fascination and curiosity as a packer whipped his bunch of heavily laden pack burros along a path near our camp. The packer's gear was much the same as I had seen since my arrival. Having just left the nearby village, the little pack burros wanted to return home more than they wanted to go down the long trail on that cold morning. It was plain to see the packer regretted not being able to stop for a visit and the coffee we offered as he dashed this way and that to keep his burros going. As the packer's shouts and the tingling of the bells grew faint in the vast emptiness of the desert beyond, I could not help but wish I could have tagged along on his journey. It would have been like stepping back into history a hundred years and seeing a way of life rapidly disappearing.

Our guide, Antonio, was a remarkable man. Proud, gracious, dignified, a father and grandfather, bow-legged with a shuffling gait characteristic of a person used to long hours in a saddle. The Indian features of his leathered face were highlighted by the universal mustache of Mexican men and a black cowboy hat. It was a pleasure to explore the secrets of that wonderful canyon country under the guidance of this sincere man.

Meredith and I watched with interest as our gear was strapped onto pack burros by two of Antonio's sons. I knew enough about the outfitting business to understand that, unless the guide asked for my assistance, the most I could do was to stay out of the way. I looked at the pack saddles, burros, and other gear with interest, noting the great differences between packing in Mexico compared to the packing I was used to in the mountain states 1,500 miles north. In a short time, we departed from the whirlwind of chickens, hogs, dogs, goats, children, and smiling, waving villagers and prepared to drop from the high plateau of the village into the rugged, silent canyons below. The only sign of wildlife I had seen was a glimpse of a fox, a scattering of birds, and the ancient, weathered antlers of a small deer hanging at an angle from a single nail in the back of a small barn. Although firearms are illegal, they have a way of appearing when needed in Mexico. I realized any game spotted was game killed in that harsh land. Still, I kept my eyes scanning the hillsides for animals, hoping to see even a remnant of former populations.

Compared to the exposed top of the plateau, the canyon bottoms offered a paradise. Much rain, by Baja standards, had recently fallen, and small streams flowed in several stretches of streambeds. Palm trees had been imported into the canyons during mission times and had overtaken the native species of trees. Just as the native trees had gradually faded from existence in the canyons, the area's native people had faded, leaving the marvelous paintings and scattered artifacts to mark their passing. The paintings themselves intrigued me. Decorating the twenty-foot-tall ceilings of long rock overhangs were dozens of larger-than-life paintings of human and animal figures. Nearly all of the paintings were done in black and red. A few of the animals were ocean dwellers, found in the salt waters, seventy five miles away. Here and there around the caves, I found small pieces of sea shells, indicating the artists who graced the caves were no strangers to long walks to the sea. In the remote, untouched depths of the canyons, where the tourist trade had not yet overrun the scene, the magic and mysticism of the paintings still held reign. A power, almost sacred in nature, flowed from the paintings. It almost seemed that the cave artists had just left for a drink of water from the nearby stream and would return at any moment.

Two of the most common animals on the cave walls we visited were bighorn sheep and branch-antlered deer. The paintings of these running animals, with spears sticking from their sides, told the story. Once these mammals were numerous enough in the area to be hunted and helped sustain a people. During our visit, only the ghosts of those people and animals remained.

Our camp that night was at a perfect oasis. Nestled on the canyon floor beside a clear pool of water, a canopy of rustling palm trees reflected our campfire's light. The riding and pack animals were hobbled with rope and turned loose to forage on the tips of bushes. There was no grass anywhere, and the ability of the domestic livestock to survive was another wonder. As with other people I had shared campfires with at a hundred locations all over the continent, we all relaxed as the soothing heat penetrated our flesh. We were no longer guides and guests. Business hours were over. We were all just fellow human beings content to pass small talk among ourselves and poke at the fire with sticks.

During our time with Antonio, I developed much respect for the man. The wisdom of his years, the knowledge gained from his experiences in the hard country of the Baja, and the integrity of his charter was of greater value than all of the gold ripped from Mexico and sent to Spain on creaking galleons. Just as the sun-baked, wind-burned, twisted mesquite trees that grew on the high hillsides, Antonio was a product of the land, irreversibly linked to its rhythms. I gained much just from watching his twinkling eyes and flame-lit face.

Antonio, man of the people. Children call to him. Antonio, man of the saddle. His spurs have jingled along many trails across the Baja. Antonio, man of the land. The canyon breeze whispers his name. Antonio. Antonio, keep care of it for all of us.

Chapter Twenty-six
Potpourri

It had been a good season. During the spring, summer, and fall, we had traveled many miles and unfolded many adventures.

In March, I took two of my horses and rode from Cheyenne, Wyoming to Denver, Colorado to attend the annual meeting of the National Wildlife Federation. The purpose of the ride was to promote and draw attention to wildlife. In my saddlebags was a letter given to me by Wyoming Govenor Mike Sullivan on the front steps of the state capitol building. I hand-delivered the letter to Colorado Govenor Roy Romer at the entrance of the conference in the heart of the mile high city.

I will always remember the ride through downtown Denver as one of the most interesting rides I ever took. I was riding Blue, my light gray gelding, who is adventurous though not aggressive. He always has a great sense of humor and the desire to break into a slow, smooth jog when possible. Behind the gelding, I led a spotted roan packhorse. The sharp clink of horseshoes striking pavement echoed loudly off of the hard sides of towering skyscrapers as we trotted our way through the bustling crowds and busy traffic of downtown Denver. Many of the people I rode past would smile, wave, ask about what we were doing, and give thumbs-up signs. Others would glance up and then stare back down at the concrete sidewalks as if they saw horses on the streets of Denver every day and were bored with them. I wouldn't recommend riding your horse through a busy city every day, but everyone should try it once!

In late April, Meredith and I turned into sailors. We launched our canoe on a particularly lovely stretch of the Green River in west central Wyoming and, three days and forty miles later, pulled our craft onto a grassy, sagebrush-covered bank that marked the end of our voyage. During the trip, we counted forty five species and thousands of individual birds. Waterfowl, blue herons, hawks, meadowlarks, ibis, and many other birds filled the land with life, color, and sound. The cottonwood-lined streambank of the river ribboned its way through the sagebrush plains and appeared much the same as it had since the first humans traveled along the river thousands of years before. It was clear by the birds' calls and activities that they were impatient for the warm days of spring.

The month of May found me working for an outdoor school and instructing two of their horsepacking courses. The students of the two horsepacking courses were like most who normally are attracted to the school—active, young, and enthusiastic people with the desire to learn as much as possible. The energy that flowed from them was contagious, their positive attitudes refreshing.

What a treat it was to show the students how to use horses and to travel through the wild places of Wyoming—places filled with history, wildlife, and unspoiled views of land not yet roaded, fenced or altered by man.

During one of the horsepacking courses, we traveled through the heart of the Red Desert in southwestern Wyoming, a fascinating place filled with incredible wonders including a desert elk herd. These elk are the same as those found in timbered mountains except that they live on the open, sagebrush-covered plains of the Red Desert. How strangely out of place these elk seemed when our horsepacking course would ride over a rolling hill and see them milling about with no trees in sight for miles in any direction. It was hard to remember that elk once lived on the open plains of North America only a few centuries ago.

The busy summer months were filled with the things that I love, the things that I live for—horsepack trips through pristine mountains where nature reigns and man is but one thread in the tapestry of life. I had horsepacking contracts to fill, plus camping and fishing trips to take with others, but I still managed to squeeze in a couple personal trips with Meredith. By the end of July, I felt tired and could see my horses were trail worn as well. Glancing at my calendar, I discovered we had been on the trail for twenty three days during the month. I allowed my horses and I the right to be a little tired.

In September, two fishing clients, Meredith, and I horsepacked to a beautiful lake surrounded on one side by towering rock cliffs, talus, and cascading waterfalls. At this place, we had an interesting adventure with bugling elk.

The weather was absolutely perfect the entire trip. Blue skies, crisp, star-filled nights, heavy frost glittering in the first rays of the morning sun. Smoke from the breakfast campfires rose straight into the air before lazily turning and drifting over the top of the thick forest below camp.

During the nights, we often were treated to the bugles of romantic-minded bull elk. We would crawl out of our warm sleeping bags at first light and take nature walks through the quiet, beckoning forest.

One morning, we crept toward the upper end of the lake where we heard the routine bugling of a mature bull. On the nearby hillside, I spotted an elk standing on an open slope. We approached within several hundred yards of the elk and paused at the edge of timber overlooking a willow-covered stream bottom. I bugled and immediately drew a bull's angry response. As the elk started walking toward us, we saw it was a handsome six-point bull with impressive, well-developed antlers.

I bugled again and the bull's reply seemed even more threatening. As we

Shotguns, pheasants, and the future of hunting are in these hunters' hands.

watched the bull descend the hill and come toward us, we were astounded to see he had only three legs. One of his hind legs was completely missing below the hock, but had long since healed. Evidently, the bull was greatly handicapped for fighting other bulls and was forced to be alone.

The bull came on. For a full five minutes, we were mesmerized as the determined bull advanced straight to our hiding place, answering loudly every bugle I offered. At fifty paces, the bull stood in short, yellow-leafed willows, balanced on his single hind leg, and bellowed clouds of steamy breath into the frosty, autumn air. Three legs or four, he was still a true monarch of the mountains.

The two anglers with me had never seen an elk before, and had doubts about being so close to such an impressive, angry animal. They seemed to be fascinated with the whole affair and, at the same time, ready to break and run for camp. I couldn't resist making a wise crack and said something to the effect that they had better get ready because the bull was going to advance to our hiding place and either fight or breed something when he arrived. The snickers my remark drew alerted the bull, and he turned and bounded away as fast as his three legs could carry him.

Perhaps one of the highlights of the year took place during the late fall. We had made our annual pilgrimage to the farms, to the brush-lined canals, weed-choked fencelines and grain fields of the lowlands for a pheasant safari.

It is important to understand the difference between a pheasant hunt and a pheasant safari. A pheasant hunt involves responsible, righteous adults using well-trained bird dogs, methodically flushing and shooting pheasants. Much decorum and strict protocol are characteristic of a pheasant hunt.

A pheasant safari, on the other hand, involves cooped-up, fun-loving kids—ranging from age seven to seventy—using well-trained bird dogs, and haphazardly crashing around in weeds and corn fields. On occasion, pheasant-safari hunters actually flush and shoot a pheasant. Wiping your runny nose with your coat sleeve is acceptable. Freshly washed and pressed shooting vests are an unknown phenomenon at pheasant safaris. Instead, shotgun shells stuffed into jean pockets is standard. Bubble gum and loud laughter are common place.

Through the years, I have learned that pheasant safaris are more fun than pheasant hunts. Pheasant hunts are normally cut-and-dried affairs, whereas pheasant safaris are always action-packed and unpredictable. Our pheasant-safari pilgrimages have included stopping en route to the field for such events as malt-tasting parties or free-style swimming contests before stewing in the hot tub of the world's largest hot spring. Oftentimes, just getting to a pheasant safari is half the fun.

That year, our pheasant-safari camp was exceptional, even by veteran hunters' standards. I arrived a few days early to reconnoiter the area for walleyes, geese, ducks, pheasants, deer, and feral pigeons. Soon after arriving, I pitched a canvas wall tent, which would serve as a kitchen, bedroom, playground, warehouse, and dog kennel. Clustered around the wall tent were duck decoys, fishing rods, a canoe, a small sleeping tent, a stack of firewood for the tin stove, a hammock stretched between two cottonwood trees, several folding chairs, a gas lantern, binoculars hanging from limbs, and other safari necessities.

What made that particular late-fall safari so special for us old kids was that the young kids came along. My brother brought his 12-year-old daughter and his much-used black labrador retriever. Our friend brought two of his young boys, ages 10 and 12, on their first pheasant safari. Without the company of the young kids, we older ones wouldn't have had nearly as much fun.

One of the reasons for that was during the weekend safari, the old kids exchanged many gifts with the young kids. We passed on to them several presents that had been given to us long ago. These gifts included the love of the outdoors, the ability to marvel at a glowing, rose-colored eastern sky just before the sun burns through the horizon, the fun of watching the alert eagerness of a bird dog when the scent becomes red hot, an understanding of the thrill and satisfaction of the one-shot killing of a fast rising bird, and the peace that comes at the end of the day when you pull the sleeping bag tight around your neck against the crisp air and recount the day's events. We hoped these gifts would serve the young kids well, last a lifetime, and again be handed along to the next generation.

In return, the children gave us gifts as well—including their vibrant laughter and their interest in and understanding of lessons from nature's outside classroom. We also enjoyed the peace of mind from seeing tired bird dogs and exhausted children snuggled together in a great, sleepy heap at the end of a day in the field.

Chapter Twenty-seven
Deer Mountain

 Twice during the late fall of 1991, Tim and I saddled our riding and packhorses in my corral, rode the ten miles to the nearby mountains above my place, and hunted for deer and elk. Tim looked for a freezer elk while we both hunted for trophy mule-deer bucks. Eventually, a dry cow elk found its way into Tim's freezer, but the big bucks we saw on the mountain still remained there after we packed our horses and headed home.

Our hunt for large buck deer was both serious and jovial. After Tim killed the dry cow the evening of the first day of hunting, the pressure to find winter's meat was eased. The search for deer became more relaxed and casual, spiced with constant jokes and laughter.

Several times, we saw bucks that converted our merriment into serious concentration. The first was a heavy-beamed, perfectly symmetrical four pointer. With meat for his family's table being a higher priority than antlers for his wall, Tim kept his .375 Winchester magnum on his shoulder and walked cautiously past the buck while stalking the elk he had seen near our camp. Later, while Tim started to dress his elk, I went looking for the buck and came within a hair of killing him as he peeked at me from behind a tree.

A second buck made the nearly mortal mistake of concentrating more on the reproductive status of the doe in front of him than on us, as we intently studied the buck's every detail from little more than a hundred yards away. The buck was just coming into his prime and had all the earmarks of growing into a big buck in future years if given the chance. We watched him as he followed the doe away.

A third buck caused me some lost sleep; the memory of his wide, towering antlers still haunts me. On a ridge above our simple horse camp just after daylight, Tim and I saw the huge buck as he escorted a doe and her fawn through a small, grassy opening, some six hundred yards away. Those who have known the thrill of seeing a buck with sweeping antlers that far exceed the width of the buck's body, know the excitement I felt as the deer slowly fed away. We immediately tried for the buck, but I missed my chance for him after, well, I was caught with my pants down. How was I to know that the buck

155

would choose the same moment to sneak back along his trail as I had chosen to answer nature's call?

A fourth large buck evaded us on the last morning of our hunt. Tim, I, and four horses had spent a snowy night at a timberline camp watching winter descend silently from a black sky. The next morning, the world was crisp, as foggy clouds moved slowly across the timbered slopes. We walked from camp just at first shooting light and traveled only a few hundred yards from camp before we started seeing deer.

On our left, Tim watched a small buck fade into nearby timber while I slowly slipped past a grazing, small buck on our right. A few minutes later, on the ridge across the valley, we spotted a buck busily checking out the plumbing of a half dozen does. The buck's antlers were just a little wider than his ears. He had four points on his left side and a deformed antler on the right that looked like a billy club with several finger-sized spikes stemming from it. We watched the activities of the deer, mapped out a plan of attack, executed our stalk excellently, and slipped up on the group of unsuspecting does only to find the clubbed-horn buck gone. As Tim approached the area where we had last seen the deer, he briefly caught sight of the buck as he vanished with a doe up a timbered mountainside.

I often wonder what stories big-game animals would tell each other if they could communicate and behave like humans after the hunting season. Imagine: The setting is a small, grass- and brush-covered hillside above a mountain watering hole. Four large bucks lie on the mountain hillside above the watering hole. One of them is a four-point deer with heavy beams and evenly matched antlers. The second deer is an average-sized buck with a slight acne problem. He chews rapidly on the food he picks from the ground and often spits out small stems.

The third buck is a true monarch with towering antlers and is agitated by the nervous spitting of the second buck. The fourth buck's face contains several old scars, his right antler is grotesquely deformed, and on his left shoulder is a heart-shaped tattoo with the word "Dear" inscribed on it. Several other deer drift to and from the watering hole and past the relaxed bucks. The four deer chew on fermented wild rose leaves, talk about does, tell about good places to eat, and visit about things important to buck deer. There is a word that describes this behavior—the deer call it buckshooting.

As the deer buckshoot each other, the topic of conversation turns toward hunting and the heavy-antlered four pointer starts a tale. "Gosh, I had a close call last season! I was staying near timberline on Hunter Creek, minding my own business, and slowly feeding below a herd of elk when all of a sudden I spotted a hunter not more than a hundred jumps away. Man, was I scared! I'll never know how he got so close before I saw him. I just pretended to keep feeding, hoping to gain some time to think. The hunter was not very tall, but carried a rifle that looked like a cannon. The barrel looked big enough for a good-sized marmot to run into. Well, sweat started dripping from my antler bases, but I noticed that the hunter seemed to be trying to ignore me and, instead, look toward the nearby elk. This suited me fine.

"As soon as the hunter passed, I hot-footed it away from there and hid in a stand of timber to see what was going to happen. Two cow elk from the herd grazed down toward where I was hiding as the hunter moved closer and closer each moment. Finally, I saw the hunter get into a shooting position, chamber a round as big around as your front leg, and murder the cow. The poor thing never knew what hit her and was dead when she hit the ground with a broken back. It's enough to make you wonder what the world is coming to!

"Back in the old days when people used to chase us around with those stone-tipped arrows and spears, it was a lot easier being a deer. There weren't so many of these blasted humans around. Even my great, great, great, great grandpa who was as near-sighted as a rock, lived to be fourteen years old before he stepped off a cliff. We figure he just didn't see it. At least he didn't have to worry about long-range ambushes like we do now.

"Anyway, no sooner had the hunter walked over to the dead elk before a second hunter joined him. Darn, I thought. The hunters talked a few moments before the first hunter pointed straight in my direction, and the second hunter started walking to the stand of trees where I was hiding. Double darn! Well, I decided to stay put for a while. I thought that if I made a break for it and was spotted, the hunter with the cannon might open up and knock a tree over on me or shake loose a landslide and crush me.

"I lost sight of the second hunter for a few minutes and thought maybe he had gone away when, all of a sudden, I could hear crunch, crunch, crunch in the snow. Thank goodness the second hunter had feet nearly as long as he was tall. He was the noisiest human I've even heard. Heck, he may as well have worn bells. I stayed put, hoping he was as blind as he was loud.

"Then, all of a sudden, when the hunter was only sixty jumps away, the crunching suddenly stopped, and my heart jumped into my throat. I peeked under a low limb of the tree I was hidden behind only to see the hunter looking at me through his binoculars. I knew I was in deep droppings, but all was not lost. The large tree in front of me covered my body and, with me peeking under the thick limb, only my nose and eyes were exposed."

At this point in the buck's narrative, a young, petite doe with large, innocent eyes daintily steps past the four bedded bucks on her way to the watering hole. The conversation ceases as the lecherous bucks leer at the doe, silly grins on their muzzles. The pock-marked buck finally can contain himself no longer and gives the deer version of a wolf whistle. The proud doe finishes her drink before lifting her nose high into the air and walking deliberately away.

The heavy-beamed buck resumes his story. "As I was saying, only my nose and eyes were exposed under the tree limb, and I ask myself what kind of a fool hunter would shoot at or could hit a deer's nose at sixty jumps. I felt fairly smug, but then the hunter calmly put his binoculars away, chambered a round in a well-used, pre '64, model 70 .270 Winchester, and pointed it directly at my nose!

"Suddenly, my left nostril began to jump and twitch in anticipation of the intrusion of a .270-caliber bullet, and I quickly raised my head to hide my nose behind the limb. The hunter responded by moving two quick steps ahead, which exposed my right shoulder to that darn Winchester. This was more than I could stand, and a lightning-fast, hard leap to my left put the tree between me and the hunter. I got out of there faster than you can say venison roast."

Protocol in buck shooting requires that a brief moment of silence transpire before any deer can say anything. During this silent period, participants' faces must remain as expressionless as a hoot owl's while all listeners carefully weigh each word of the previous speaker. After an appropriate amount of time, the scar-faced buck with the deformed antler and tattoo speaks: "You were lucky. That was a close call. I almost ran into those same two hunters earlier. The only thing that saved me was that my dear old doe friend, Lilly, and I decided to leave early just before those two yo-yos came up. I told Lilly I wanted to show her some of my newest buck rubs up on Solitary Ridge, and she agreed to go. What a great doe. They don't make 'em like her anymore. She sure has a crush on me!"

"Well, it's probably because of your good looks," the handsome monarch says sarcastically. The club-antlered buck starts to counter the cutting remark, but stops as his eyes rivet on the huge, impressive antlers of the monarch. "I, too, had a close encounter with those same hunters," continues the monarch. "I found that they were quite easy to evade. Even before daylight on the day I saw them, I knew hunters were in the area. With their disgusting smells, noisy horses, and their constant bursts of laughter, their presence was well announced.

"I chose to climb to my favorite bed under a large tree, halfway up Coronary Ridge. From there, I can see far in all directions, and I spotted the two hunters looking for me. It was amusing to watch them hopelessly search. I personally do not credit the pair much for their hunting finesse, especially the tall one who looked like a scarecrow on water skis. It was when that one had his rifle well out of reach and his pants down around his ankles that I decided to slip away from those clowns. Of course, I showed myself briefly as I departed, just to humiliate them. Perhaps by next year they will decide that some other sport may be more rewarding than trying to match wits with me."

Despite the humiliation, the memories that Tim and I have from those days on the mountain will draw us back next year to look for big buck deer. Perhaps after our return from that hunt, the stories around the watering holes will be different!

Chapter Twenty-eight
A Different Kind of Trophy

 On my wall hang two mule-deer antlers. One is bleached white from laying in the sun while the other still shows its dark walnut color. Each rack has four points, though completely different. To anyone else, they would appear to be no different from any of the antlers commonly piled in people's yards. To me, though, they are treasures, reminders of a special hunt, and worthy substitutes for the big buck I sought but failed to kill.

Most people cannot comprehend my fascination with antlers or the many things they mean to me. They know only that I found the shed antlers while hunting deer in southern Utah. They don't understand how ardently I had dreamed for years of returning to that land of junipers, oak brush, thick mountain-mahogany jungles, aspen and pine groves clinging to the higher peaks, and sandstone bluffs above winding canyonlands that echo the scream of the sleek mountain lion. These lands held me spellbound as I traveled through them in years past.

Those who don't understand know nothing of the friendships with former Utah residents, which led to the opportunity to stalk the well-used deer trails, nor were they present when we drove from Wyoming, toured the sights in Salt Lake City, and wheeled south to the canyon lands. There is no way to share with others the fun we had, the joking among new and old friends gathered at our huge, lantern-lit tent at night, or the bursts of laughter we emitted as we escaped from the pressures of the working world and let off steam. We were as carefree as kids at camp. People think it odd when I look at those antlers and grin, barely able to contain a chuckle at the recollections of good times.

The shed antlers give no hint of the surprised look on my face when I saw our campsite and the size of the crowd assembled there. It is hard for people to comprehend how appalled I, the veteran of dozens of wilderness camps, was at the sight of scores of neighboring motor homes, trailers, and assorted recreational vehicles. Noisy off-road vehicles buzzed everywhere. Our camp alone had ten vehicles, two horse trailers, eight horses, three camper trailers, two tents, a portable electric generator, and a litter of six-week-old hounds. A rifle range was set up beside the camp, and many hunters checked their rifles the afternoon before deer season opened. I imagined no deer would be so foolish as to be anywhere within twenty miles of our camp on opening morning. How wrong I was. The shed antlers are reminders that I did not give up completely at the sight of all the commotion.

Instead, I followed the lead of the veterans and joined in the carnival atmosphere.

The antlers bring back memories of the incredible swirl of hunters and deer on the hillsides on opening day. It's difficult to say whether deer, hunters, or rifle shots were more abundant. Each could be counted by the hundreds. I am reminded of finding a vantage point and watching many does, fawns, and a half dozen small bucks trot past. At the end of the day, I was stunned when I realized the number of deer I had seen—well over a hundred. I recall being lured for several days by a remote, rough mountain where few hunters ventured. There, I thought, was the hiding place of the heavy-antlered buck I sought. The dangerous rockslides, the silent aspen groves, and the mountain mahogany thickets were ideal components of a big buck's stronghold.

The buck was there. I saw his legs, thicker and darker than those of the small bucks and does I had seen, below the bottom limbs of a juniper tree. He knew danger was close as he stood two hundred yards away, shielded by the tree. My crosshairs probed for a patch of hair among the thick boughs, but none appeared large enough for a target. Several times, the buck swung his head, and I saw sunlight reflect off his thick shiny beams. After five minutes of suspense, he took two steps and vanished into the brushy hillside. The buck had won.

The sight of the shed antlers has helped me count my lucky stars. I am thankful for the opportunity to test myself against wary bucks; not many on this planet have that privilege. It is gratifying to think of the autumn when I hunted antelope in Wyoming, elk in Colorado, and deer in Utah. This good fortune was not the result of monetary wealth. It came about because I chose to hunt on my own for wild game on public lands.

The shed antlers are a strange trophy. Although meaningless to others, they are like magic wands to me, able to whisk my thoughts to a brush-covered canyonland teeming with deer. Their powers never fail to raise my spirits and call for my return to the big bucks in the canyonlands of Utah and all the other places where I have been privileged to share the habitat of our magnificent game animals.